GERALD
GOD AND THE DJ

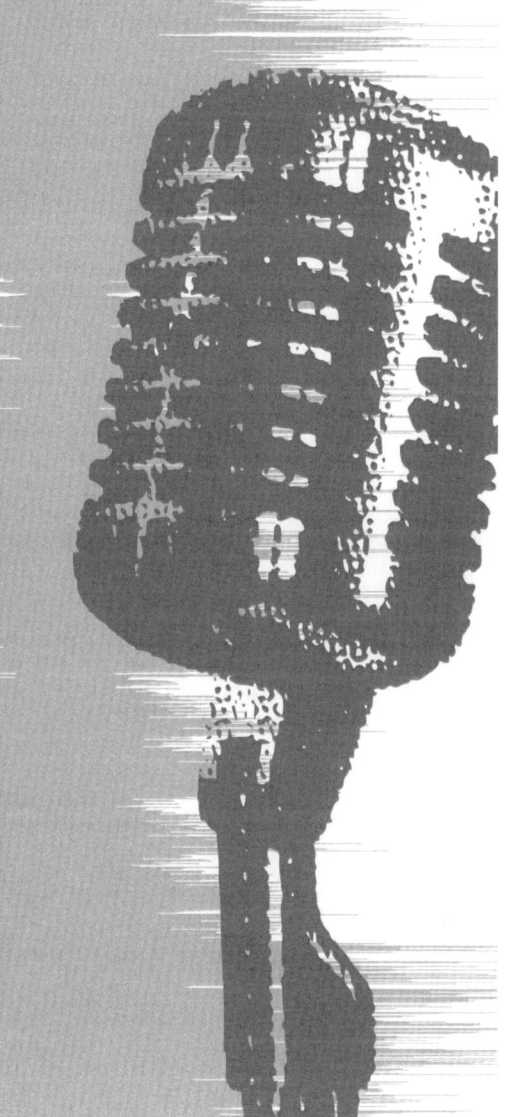

THE OWENS PUBLISHING
— COMPANY —

God & The DJ
By Gerald McBride

Copyright © 2025 by Gerald McBride
Printed in the United States of America

ISBN: 979-8-9922925-5-8

All rights reserved solely by the author. The author guarantees all contents are original and do not infringe upon the legal rights of any other person or work. No part of this book may be reproduced in any form without the permission of the author. The views expressed in this book are not necessarily those of the publisher.

www.OwensPublishingCompany.com

DEDICATION

To my dearly beloved wife, Karen:

Your love for me has been God-sent. Thank you for the joy and laughter you have brought into my life every single day since we have been together.

Thank you for the encouragement you have always given me to work harder, for the faith you have shown in me to believe in myself more than ever, and for your strength that pushes me to never stop for a pity party. I mean it when I joke that if I told you I wanted to be an astronaut, you would make me a glass of Tang and buy me a space helmet!

You are the woman behind this man's success. There have been many times in our praise and worship together at church or at home when the presence of God would come down so strong that I would hear the voice of the Lord telling me, "With this woman, you are in my perfect will."

For inspiring me to be more, Karen, I dedicate this book to you.

Yours for all eternity,

Gerald

Acknowledgments

First and foremost, I give all glory and honor to God, who authored every step of this journey long before I ever imagined writing a book. His guidance, His timing, and His grace have carried me through every page.

A deeply heartfelt thanks to my pastor, **Dominic Russo**. Pastor, God has used you in mighty ways to guide, nurture, and strengthen my faith. Your words of encouragement have reached me at moments only Heaven understood. Through your sermons, your counsel, and the quiet moments of prayer we've shared, you helped awaken a deeper faith within me, stretching my spirit and lifting me to places I never imagined possible. Thank you for being a compassionate shepherd, for speaking truth in love, and for always challenging me to grow into the calling God placed on my life.

To my beloved family - **Jaz, Brandy, Dway, Alana, Daniel**, and my two precious grandchildren, **Tandie and Cooper Mitchell**, you are God's greatest earthly blessings to me. Your love is my joy, your support is my anchor, and your presence makes life not only worth living, but worth celebrating. Thank you for believing in me, standing with me, and filling my life with purpose and laughter.

In sacred memory of my dear cousin, **Donna Kay**. Donna Kay, when you asked me to write a few lines for a family album, neither of us knew that God was planting the very seed of this book. Your life radiated

Christ's love, your joy, your laughter, your compassion, and your unwavering encouragement touched countless hearts. You were more than a cousin; you were a true sister in Christ whose influence shaped my journey. Now that you are in the presence of the Lord, reunited with our loved ones, I know you have heard those cherished words: *"Well done, My good and faithful servant."* Your legacy lives on in these pages.

To **The Owens Publishing Company - Dawn Owens**, a heartfelt thank you to you and your husband, Jesse. As this is my very first book, I truly believe God placed me with the perfect team for this assignment. Your encouragement gave me the confidence to move forward and share my story with boldness. Working with you has felt divinely ordered; our connection, our conversations, and the purpose behind this project were aligned by God's timing. Our deep talks about faith, expression, and calling helped shape this book in ways I never could have anticipated. I look forward to many more projects together. May God continue to bless you, Jesse, your family, and The Owens Publishing Company with abundant favor, growth, and vision.

And to all of my **radio listeners around the world**, thank you for allowing me to share musical memories with you for more than four decades. You welcomed me into your homes, your cars, your celebrations, and your quiet moments. My radio career has been a gift, and it is because of your loyalty and love that every show felt like family. I am forever grateful for your support.

TABLE OF CONTENTS

Dedication iii
Acknowledgments v
Introduction 1
Chapter 1 — Twinkling Stars of Inkster 5
Chapter 2 — Music and Family 13
Chapter 3 — A New Chapter In Detroit 19
Chapter 4 — Mumford High School 31
Chapter 5 — Post-High School Years & Many Firsts 43
Chapter 6 — My Radio Journey 53
Chapter 7 — The Big Breaks. 63
Chapter 8 — God Help Me 79
Chapter 9 — TV Shows 87
Chapter 10 — My Big Bold Steps 93
Chapter 11 — Struggles and Turning Points. 101
Chapter 12 — Legacy Born in a Small Apartment 109
Chapter 13 — Our Black Entertainment 117
Chapter 14 — The Future of Now 127
Chapter 15 — Faith & Good Fortunes 141
Chapter 16 — Lockdown Lessons & Leadings 149
Chapter 17 — Purpose 159
Chapter 18 — Black Ice. 169
Chapter 19 — A Life of Meaning 177
Chapter 20 — It's a Wrap!. 185
About the Author. 205

Introduction

There are several decisions that shape the life of a man, as we are faced with many choices, both great and small. Yet, in the midst of all the thousands of decisions I have had to make in my lifetime, there is none that will ever compare to the moment I turned my life over to Jesus Christ. Though born and raised in a Catholic Christian family, it was in my mid-30s that I truly answered the call of my Lord and Savior, and it has been a journey of faith since then.

After I received the gracious salvation of Christ, I have had the privilege to hear from the Lord in an unmistakably clear manner. In each of these times that the Lord has spoken to me, I always had the strong urge to journal these conversations. I mean, think about it, here is the creator of the entire universe speaking to you, wouldn't you want to write down His instructions so that you will never forget His words, even as time passes and memories fade?

The journal entries of my conversations with God have been a source of immense strength to me several times when I was weakened by fear, defeat, and failure. I just needed to go back and reflect on what the Lord said to me, and then I would be renewed and feel encouraged, as if I were hearing those reassuring words of the Lord anew. Every single time, I became blessed by His conversations all over again.

This book is a biography of my journey through life, and I have shared both my mistakes and successes in the hopes that every reader will find inspiration, courage, and wisdom from the decisions I made over the span of more than fifty years. Moreover, more than learning from the life experiences I will share with you, I will also write the comforting words that God spoke to me through my highs and lows. I believe these intimate instructions and words of affirmation will bless you greatly as you consciously apply them to your life as well.

As I am writing this, I can hear the Lord clearly saying to me, "Gerald, please share these things; you know my voice. These words will confirm just how much I love them as well."

And truly, I know HIS voice. So, here am I, sharing these words of life as I take you through events and lessons of my life.

Things God Spoke to Me:

*"Don't you know I'm here, Gerald?
I am here, so you don't have to fight.
You only have to trust me. For this is my battle.
Be where I want you to be. Say what I want you to say.
I know the plans I have for you. Follow me and learn my voice.
You are my faithful servant.
Trust me, Gerald. Do not get off track.
Stay in the secret place, for this is where battles are won.
I have a great plan for your life. Wait on me. Don't be anxious.
Trust me, Gerald. Rest in me."*

Chapter One

Twinkling Stars of Inkster

It was the summer of 1962 in Inkster, Michigan. The neighborhood was alive with activity—hammocks swayed on front porches in the gentle breeze, flowers bloomed in the gardens, and JFK was president of the United States.

Motown music filled our small, one-story brick house, which looked nearly identical to all the others on our block. From the large black radio which sat on a wooden shelf, a deep, familiar voice announced, "You are listening to the Black Giant WCHB Inkster!" This was followed by the sounds of Marvin Gaye singing, *"Say yeah yeah yeah, say yeah yeah yeah!"* as his hit song *Stubborn Kinda Fella* set the upbeat atmosphere in our home.

I was born and raised in the Annapolis Park neighborhood on Hanover Street in Inkster. Rumor has it that the city of Inkster was built upon land purchased by the great Henry Ford. He wanted to help provide jobs for the African Americans who were migrating from the South to the North to work in his factory, which was just a few miles away in Dearborn, Michigan. The city was also named after Ford's favorite singing group, the Ink Spots. Back in '62, Inkster was one of his favorite places, and indeed, it was a booming automotive city, just like other parts of Detroit, Michigan.

I was five years old, and the youngest of four boys. My brothers, Andy, David, and Reggie, called me "The Thumb Sucker," a nickname I earned because I couldn't keep my thumb out of my mouth. Andy and David teased and laughed at me, but Reggie treated the thumb like a deadly disease, running for cover anytime I brought the thumb near him. Hence, every other day, I would chase Reggie around the house with my thumb, and he would scream and run around the house for protection against the threat of my deadly wet big finger.

My father, Andrew McBride, was a graduate of Tuskegee University and worked as an electrical engineer for HF Campbell, a firm based in Dearborn, Michigan, while my mother, Marvine McBride, was a stay-at-home mom who had her hands full with four kids.

Our house was near an airport. I remember running around the living room with my brother Reggie, who was closest to me in age, terrified and screaming in delight and fright. You see, whenever the loud plane engines roared and the shadow from the wings cast darkness over our house, it was an event.

* * *

In 1963, we moved across town to Penn Street. People who lived in Inkster considered this "living across the road," meaning you lived on the other side of Inkster Road, the main street that divided the city.

As quiet as it was kept, the two sides had a rivalry against one another, which I could never understand for such a small city.

History knows that Detroit, Michigan, and its suburb of Inkster were the hub for some of the best R&B music in the country, mainly because this was Motown. Back in the 1960s, radio stations like WCHB in Inkster, whose radio signal would reach Detroit, were absolutely crucial to the rise and success of Motown music, almost like the "oxygen" that let the sound breathe into every home, car, and street corner in the city. Berry Gordy's Motown label started in 1959, and local Black radio was one of the *first* to embrace the label's artists before they broke nationally. The DJs weren't just spinning records; they were tastemakers. Their style, humor, and swagger influenced how people experienced the music.

Many Motown artists, including Smokey Robinson, The Supremes, and Stevie Wonder, remembered hearing their own records played by these DJs and even dropping by the station for interviews.

Radio airplay also meant that Motown's crossover appeal could be tested: WCHB built a base in the Black community, and once songs were proven hits there, they could be pitched to white Top 40 stations like CKLW.

Every morning, our large radio would wake us up, its sound blasting into every room of our house. During afternoons, disc jockey Bill Williams would introduce himself with his signature phrase: "This is Still Bill Williams on your radio!"

In the evenings, a different announcer would enthusiastically say, "Here is the 12-year-old genius. They call him Little Stevie Wonder..." Then, Little Stevie would sing, *"Everybody say yeah...!!!"*

As we moved from Hanover to Penn Street, "across the road," these familiar sounds and voices became the daily soundtrack of our new home. I could write a book on my father's life, but one thing that stood out about him was that he had vision. We moved to this old farmhouse on the other side of town. It sat on two acres of wooded land. The house was worn, rickety, and in very bad condition, but the scenery that surrounded our home was breathtaking. The front lawn was lush and green, providing a perfect playground for my brothers and me, who loved to run around and roll on the bare ground. The woods behind the house looked like a well-kept garden, and thanks to my dad's vision and excellent carpentry skills, both sides of the house were fascinating to me even as a kid.

My younger sister, Julie, came into the world shortly after we moved to Penn Street, and my dad built her a beautiful crib in a middle room connected to my parents' bedroom. When Julie was about eight months old, my mother took in a stray black cat. Mom had started out with just feeding the cat on the front porch before eventually allowing the cat to stay in the house. We were all asleep in the house one night when the cat jumped into Julie's crib. By the next morning, when we all woke up, my baby sister's sheets had red blood stains all over them. And she was surrounded by eight newborn kittens! The mother cat had given birth to her kittens right beside my baby sister, who was subsequently (and affectionately) known as the original Cat Woman!

Almost always, I would wake up in the morning to find my dad sitting at the kitchen table with a sketch pad and a pencil. Every now and then, his eyes would linger on the wall or ceiling as he stared into space, imagining different styles of designs that he could create for the run-down country house we lived in. My father, being from Ripley, Tennessee, learned his carpentry skills from his uncle, Johnny McBride, who was also a great carpenter. Johnny had allowed my dad to shadow him when my father was young. Some days, he would wake up at dawn to measure the length of the rooms as he imagined different ways to remodel our house.

Whenever I looked through my dad's sketches, I was always impressed by the sheer brilliance in his artwork. I would see the rough architectural designs of the kitchen with dimensions of height and length, and accurate measurements all laid out on his notepad. Then, like some sort of miracle for my young mind, a few days later, I would wake up to the sound of demolition by my dad's one-man operation. The next thing I knew, walls would get torn down and cabinets taken out.

In a few hours' time, the area my dad had worked on would become completely transformed into the exact design I had seen as a sketch inside the notepad on the kitchen table. In my eyes, my father was a genius when it came to architecture and design. This is probably why I always had the desire to build something or at least remodel something in the homes I have owned over the years, though I was never quite as good as my dad when it came to these skills. Within the first year of moving into the old, worn house on Penn Street, my dad had turned the rickety structure into a nice place for his family to call home, or at least, that was what my young mind thought at the time. That is, if you think that the idea of four boys sleeping in one bedroom works just fine! Regardless, I had some of the best childhood memories of my life while living in our house in Inkster.

My family embraced every opportunity to explore and have an adventure. We spent hours hiking through the woods behind our house with pathways that led to a big park on the other side. The park had swings, slides, merry-go-rounds, a baseball diamond, a full football field, and so many more exciting attractions, and it was here that my brothers and I spent most of our days. Our house also had a huge basement, and I remember several Cub Scout meetings held there with my mother acting as den mother for my group.

At lunchtime, my older teenage brothers, David and Andy, who were now 14 and 17, would invite their friends from high school to come by and hang out in the basement, and my mother would fix her famous 'Mama McBride hamburgers' wrapped in wax paper, dripping with grease. It didn't take much time before word got around about the lunchtime get-together that was happening in our basement. The crowd grew larger and larger until the basement became a place where a crowd of teenagers gathered to dance to Motown music and eat some great burgers for .15 cents each.

When *Mr. Mets*, the restaurant that had just opened across the street from our house, caught wind of what was happening, they quickly offered my mom a job to work in the restaurant and add her famous burgers to the menu. Like bees to a honeycomb, the crowd moved out of our basement to the new burger hangout at *Mr. Mets*.

My brothers were always in singing groups and would have many rehearsals in our basement. Motown music was on a tremendous rise at this time in American history, and so many of the folks in Inkster wanted to become the next big star. Andy was a very talented singer and bass player, and he was always with his friends in the basement, rehearsing the Temptations' choreography and songs in preparation for the local talent shows. I always thought Andy's moves were so smooth. He even went one step further and processed his hair to look like a legitimate member of the actual Temptations.

One of my mother's best friends was Shirley Sharpley, who lived just a few blocks away. We spent a lot of time at the Sharpley's house, playing with their kids, Stevie and Lora Lynn. Shirley Sharpley was a school teacher at Inkster High School. One year during the 1960s, she noticed a singing group of four girls who won the Inkster High School talent show with their sharp harmony and choreography. Shirley was so impressed that she took it upon herself to contact Berry Gordy to inform him about these talented young girls who had performed at her school. With her persistence, they were granted an audition that would eventually lead to a recording contract. They became the "Marvelettes," who would go on to become one of Motown's biggest groups, making numerous hits like "Please, Mr. Postman," "Don't Mess with Bill," and many more.

* * *

As usual, I woke up one morning to the strong smell of coffee brewing in the kitchen. I found my way to the living room as I always did and saw my mother and father sipping from their cups of coffee. When I looked around the room, a man in his mid-twenties was lying on the couch, fast asleep. I frowned and looked at my parents for an explanation, but they paid no attention to me. "Who is this?" I thought, but I knew better than to ask my parents questions about things considered to be grown folks' business. So, I quietly left the room.

When the man woke up later that morning, I noticed that my mom was being really nice to him. He was also very nice to me and my brothers, as he handed some cash to each of us. It was then that I realized this stranger was not so strange at all. I had seen a few pictures of him around the house, dressed in an army uniform, standing next to a tank. I remember his face because I always thought the man in the picture was so cool. Could this be the same person in the pictures? How do I ask? Who do I ask?

This mystery clouded my mind for a few days until Andy finally explained. The stranger in the army uniform was our eldest brother, and his name was Marvin Figgins. My mom had him from a previous relationship when she was 16 years old. I believe it was something my older brothers knew, but I must have been too young to comprehend.

He was at our house because his home in Detroit had caught fire, and Marvin needed someplace for his family to stay. He spoke with my parents, and they agreed to have them stay with us.

I will never forget the day his entire family arrived. The smell of smoke was so pungent in their clothes and belongings that our entire house smelled like smoke. This would be my first introduction to my nieces, who were close in age to me. The two girls, Timeko and Michelle, had such beautiful smiles, just like their mom, Roma, who was a beautiful woman with a 60s hairstyle and a mod dress style that reminded me of one of the Motown Supremes. It always surprised me to see how cheerful they were despite losing their house in the fire.

This was the first time I learned that faith and joy can abide despite tough life situations.

Things God spoke to me:

"Know that I am ordering your steps in so many ways.
Yes, I have heard your prayers.
Just walk in the divine favor I have for you today.
Have confidence in the Holy Spirit I have provided
for you.
You'll always know what to say because of the greater one
that lives inside of you.
You have acknowledged me in many ways,
Now I shall acknowledge you.
Trust me, Gerald. Go on trusting me."

Chapter Two

Music and Family

In 1965, my mother continued her habit of keeping the radio tuned to her beloved station, the Black Giant WCHB, which played nonstop throughout our home. By now, I recognized the voices of the radio DJs and knew their names by heart. Butterball Jr., Bill Williams, Paul Childs, Fred Goree, Jay Butler, and even the newsman, Marvin Moss! All of these men were radio stars in Inkster, and they were legends in my eyes. Inkster was an all-black community with a black-owned radio station and other black businesses like Mr. Alan's Supermarket, Kirk's BBQ, Stardust Lounge, and many others.

Growing up in an all-black city meant that I never really experienced racism, and frankly speaking, I didn't see any differences between me and every other human. The majority of people I knew were black, and when I saw white or brown folks, their skin color never mattered. They were just people, like me, and that was it.

Well, everything changed when the world showed me another side of human nature. Our house stood on the corner of Penn Street and Beech Daly, which was on the border of Dearborn Heights and Inkster. Andy and David attended Robichaud High School, which was a few blocks away in Dearborn Heights. At this time, about ninety percent of the students in Robichaud were white, with only a handful of blacks from Inkster who were required to attend this school because of city regulations.

I was on the front porch of our house one day when I saw a group of black teenage students running for the Inkster border. They were being chased home from school by a crowd of angry white boys holding steel chains, throwing glass bottles, and hurling rocks at the black kids who were trying to make their way to Inkster for safety. My brothers, Andy and David, were part of the group of black students being chased, and they barely escaped the mob. As soon as my brothers crossed the border onto Beech Daly Street, the group of angry white kids stood at the border, throwing rocks and shouting racial slurs at the fleeing black students. This was my first introduction to racism.

We would also take family trips to my father's hometown of Ripley, Tennessee. The trips with all five of us in my father's long Cadillac would usually happen around Easter during our spring breaks from school. While we were there, we learned a lot of family history from my Aunt Dorothy and my grandparents on my father's side, David and Earlie McBride. They often shared fascinating stories about life in the South, my father's childhood, and the McBride family line.

Like most lineages of African Americans, our roots were traced back to our great-grandfather, John McBride, who was half white as a result of a slave master who got one of his slaves pregnant. One day, during a stroll through the small downtown of Ripley, Tennessee, with my grandfather, we sat in the town center where my grandfather fed the pigeons with peanuts from his pocket. As I looked up, I noticed a sign on the front of a laundromat door that read "Whites Only." I would never forget the image of that sign on the door that helped my young mind understand that racism was real and that there was a difference between how others saw me and themselves.

* * *

Andy kept on growing his style of music, and the Temptations were still his heroes. I remember hearing some voices in the basement one day and heading down there to listen to Andy and his friends. It was quite clear at this time that Andy was gifted at singing, and I loved listening to his voice. When I entered the basement, Andy was holding an LP with five brown-skinned guys on the cover; all five of them looked like they were brothers. The title on the LP cover read "Meet the Temptations," and Andy's friends gathered around the record as he put the needle onto the vinyl. As the song began with that famous Motown guitar riff, the five brothers sang the lyrics in the most perfect harmony I had ever heard.

"*You got a smile so bright...*" The five boys softly sang... "*You know you could have been a candle...*" Andy joined the singing as the lead voice, and David backed him up with tenor. As I listened and watched the guys, pride welled up within me; I became certain that music would become a part of our family's future.

Our house was always filled with music. Reggie was eight when he started showing some interest in music. Every morning, when we sat at the table for breakfast, Reggie would hold the cereal box and read the words written on it, and with each spoonful he put into his mouth, he would hum some unknown tune and bang on the table in pleasure as if he was playing drums. This always drove me crazy, but Reggie found great pleasure in this little act, and he never stopped creating music from anything he could find.

When he was ten, Reggie asked my mother to buy him a guitar, but Mom didn't take him seriously. Since she ignored his request, he decided to make his own guitar. Reggie got an old Tide Box, some rubber bands, and an old broomstick. He bound the band to the broomstick, fixed both onto the box, and made himself a homemade guitar. He would play at the rubber bands as if they were guitar strings, and he enjoyed the sound that came from his creation. Naturally, this touched my mother's heart, and before long, she bought Reggie a guitar and signed him up for weekly lessons. My mother always showed her support for any of our interests. She went far and beyond to make sure we felt loved, and she always did her best to encourage us in the arts and entertainment.

Needless to say, Reggie learned the guitar quickly and excelled at it. Since Reggie only had one guitar, his teacher changed the tone of the guitar to make it sound like a bass. And this was how Reggie transitioned to playing the bass guitar. By the age of eleven, Reggie joined his first band, a group of boys called "The Matadors." I will never forget seeing him in one of his first talent shows doing a bass guitar solo of *Tighten Up*, a popular song by Archie Bell and the Drells. Reggie played the bass solo with such precision that the crowd went wild. It was at this point that we all realized that Reggie had something special.

Musical talent has always been in my family's genes. My grandfather, David McBride, played guitar in a band, and my aunt, Dorothy, played the piano and sang for her church. With my mother's passion for music, she was determined to spark our musical interest in her own way. She did her best to make all of us pick up an instrument. Personally, she always loved the sound of the Hammond B3 organ, so she bought me a small toy organ as a Christmas gift. Unfortunately, I never got the hang of playing the organ, nor did I feel the desire to dedicate any time to learn or practicing.

Discovering the real talent that her first three children had displayed in music, my mother did her best to get my sister and me into learning an instrument. One day, we found out that our mother had signed us up for accordion lessons when a man arrived at the house with a suitcase. Mom told us he was there for our lessons, and Julie and I were thrilled at the idea. But the lessons didn't last for more than a few weeks before the man stopped coming. Neither of us was really sure why the lessons stopped; either we were so bad at learning the accordion, or my mother just wasn't feeling that type of music.

Watching Andy, David, and Reggie showcase their musical talents often made me question whether I possessed some untapped musical ability waiting to be discovered. I always thought that maybe if Julie and I had kept at it, we might have become the first-ever funky African-American accordion players. And to this day, I still ask myself, if I spend time learning and practicing, could I master an instrument? I expressed this to my wife recently, and what did she do? She went out and bought me a beautiful guitar, of course.

All through my childhood, going to church was one of my favorite things to do. It wasn't exactly a family tradition—my father and brothers rarely went with us. Most Sundays, it was just me, Julie, and my mother attending our Catholic church in Inkster, where I especially loved the Sunday mass.

My mother held a special place in her heart for God and deeply desired for all of us to experience His presence. For me personally, these weekly gatherings instilled a deep reverence for God. I felt certain that God existed and watched over me. I was always excited to give at offering time and take the communion.

My devotion ran so deep that I once promised my mother I would become a priest someday. There was something grand and reverent about the priestly role that captivated me. Naturally, my mother was thrilled by this declaration, as she had always hoped we would develop a closer relationship with God. Besides, Mom was always supportive when she saw that we were excited to do something good.

This was one of the most crucial parenting skills I learned from my mother. It is always important for parents to notice the little things their children say about their dreams, passions, and futures. The parents' role is to guide and help develop these passions into something meaningful and profound.

Things God spoke to me:

*I am so pleased that you trust me, Gerald.
I am leading the way, so keep trusting me.
You will become an example of my goodness.
Trust me, and I will show you the way to go.
People must know that I exist.
You have become my messenger.
Show them my love. Never stop being generous.
That is who I made you to be.*

Chapter Three

A NEW CHAPTER IN DETROIT

I always knew my father was highly skilled at his job. He was a genius in my eyes as a kid, and the dexterity with which he came up with design ideas always left me in awe of his talent. Therefore, it didn't surprise me when Dad came home one day in the spring of 1969 and announced he had gotten a new job in Detroit. The new job offered much higher pay, and I celebrated the news just like the rest of the family. However, it was a few days later that I realized the significance of this great news. We were all going to move out of Inkster.

Everything I knew and loved was in Inkster. Needless to say, I was no longer so enthused by the news of my father's new job. When Mom told me we were moving to Detroit so Dad wouldn't live too far from work, I pleaded with her not to take me away from Inkster. My pleas didn't matter, however. Shortly after Dad got the new job, the Inkster city council offered my dad sixteen thousand dollars to sell the house to the city. The property was beautiful and sat in the middle of the park, so the city wanted to pull down the old house and expand the park. The money was too attractive and significant to refuse.

Dad sold the house and used the money to buy a more secure, newer property on the west side of Detroit. Our new home was in the Detroit University district, a short distance from my father's new office. Our new house had all the modern designs, and my room was far more spacious than the one in the old house, but these aesthetics didn't give me much comfort. I was sad to leave Inkster, my friends, and the enjoyment of the outdoors and park lifestyle I had become accustomed to.

Detroit had all the advantages and temptations of a modern city. The streets were wide, the sidewalks were painted white, and the alleys had several turns and corners where kids could play. My brothers were only too pleased to move into this vibrant new environment. It didn't take long before they knew all the popular spots and found places for themselves in the city. Without the basement and my brothers' music that made the house in Inkster quite interesting, the new house in Detroit felt dull in comparison. Dad worked more and now spent more time outdoors, and my brothers found their places elsewhere in the city. I was often in the house alone with Mom, Julie, and Reggie. For me, a boy plucked from his friends and familiar surroundings, this transition was a huge adjustment, and I became less extroverted.

Our Detroit neighborhood in the University District was not the all-black community that Inkster was, and this new reality needed getting used to. Our new neighborhood was predominantly Jewish, with a few black families who were just moving in like we were. Hence, I couldn't shake the feeling of uneasiness in this new place. I was so frustrated with the strangeness of this new environment that I walked up to my mother after lunch one afternoon with a request.

"Ma," I began, hesitantly, "I want to go back to Inkster."

My mother was too amused to respond. She kept turning over the dishes in the kitchen sink.

"I promise I won't be any trouble, Ma," I pestered, suddenly finding the courage to speak more. "I will live with Lem. His folks will allow me to stay with them."

Mom started rinsing the dishes.

"I can come and visit here during weekends if you want," I continued. "I promise I won't be any trouble, Ma."

When my mother finally turned to answer me. Her eyes were filled with compassion, but her voice was firm. "We are a family," she said. "We will live here together. This is our home now," Mom added in a tone that suggested the conversation had come to an end.

I had a lot to say, but I decided it was better to keep quiet. Mom was a kind woman who supported us a lot, but we all had the quiet understanding that she could be strict whenever she chose.

I wasn't the only one struggling with the new reality. About two months after we moved to Detroit, I started noticing that my father was gone a lot more often. As his business grew and he took on more electrical contracting jobs, his working hours also became longer. Typically, he would leave the house shortly after dawn and wouldn't come back until late in the evening, when I had gone to bed. A full week could pass, and I would only see my father on the nights I stayed up too late. And in those few times when he returned before I slept, he had become louder than I knew him to be.

As the months went by, I finally understood that my father had developed a serious drinking problem. On several nights, he would get into serious arguments with my mom, and their voices would get so loud that it would wake me up. The reason for the fight was always the same... my mother strongly disagreed with my father's new habit. He was getting home too late because he stopped at the local bar that was just up the street and drank away his hard-earned money.

Despite his drinking problem, my father continued to be brilliant at his job. There were many times when other electricians and contractors from all over Detroit would come by the house to seek his advice and get ideas on their own jobs. And my father always helped them out with his suggestions and strategies. This only happened when these contractors came to the house at the right time, though. If they showed up late in the evening when my father had had one drink too many, his words of advice would get so blurred by intoxication that it would be impossible to understand whatever he had to say.

I also benefited greatly from my father's intelligence as I often waited up for him to help me with homework. He was quite helpful with the technical subjects, especially mathematics and the sciences. However, just as those contractors did, I needed to ask for his help when his mind was clear. If I asked for his help when he was already drunk, the session would quickly become a shouting match, with him correcting and criticizing me in a harsh, angry tone.

"You don't know how to solve this problem"? He would often ask. "How come you don't get this?"

My lips would quiver when he spoke harshly like this, and my eyes would quickly well up. And this would almost always cause a reaction from him. As time went on, I started keeping my homework from my dad, which meant I struggled to understand several topics, particularly in algebra.

This went on for a while until my father's lack of patience and understanding eroded my confidence in my academic ability, and for years, I falsely assumed that I had a learning disability. Because I didn't do well on my assignments and my dad's comments about me not understanding seemingly simple questions, I concluded that I wasn't smart enough. It took about two decades before I finally accepted that I was a smart kid who just had an impatient teacher.

Parents have the greatest impact on their kids through the words they speak. We all must encourage our children in every area of their lives and understand that our words have power. Parents are the biggest influences in their kids' lives, and we are the people they admire and listen to the most. Invariably, if you constantly tell your kids they are not smart, they will start to believe it and act it out. On the other hand, if positive affirming words are spoken to the child, they will reflect these positive qualities as they learn and grow up. Proverbs 18:21 expressly declares that "Death and Life are in the power of the tongue, and those who love it will eat its fruit." All parents, teachers, guardians, and counselors must understand that they must only speak life over children.

We moved from Inkster to Detroit during the Christmas break, so I didn't resume in my new school until January 6th, 1970. Hampton Junior High had bigger classrooms, buildings with better architectural design, a more modern gym, and much stricter teachers.

Everything in this new school seemed to move on at double speed, and I couldn't keep up with the lessons and expectations. The school was rowdy to say the least. For example, in my first week, some students started a fire, but no one got hurt. However, school wasn't *all* bad. I knew two brothers who also moved from Inkster and attended the school. It took some time, but I eventually settled in and adapted to the school's pace. I made a few friends in my homeroom class, and some of them are still my friends today.

Despite being in a predominantly white neighborhood, Hampton Junior High had more black students than white students. Most of the students lived outside the University District, on the other side of Livernois, and in other black neighborhoods like 8 Mile and Pembroke. One of the big shocks I got in my time in Hampton was the high rate and degree of bullying that existed in the school. If you think bullying started just recently, you might have to think again. There was a guy in my homeroom class, Norman Montgomery, who had everyone scared. He made it his duty to bully each member of the class one by one. He would accost people unprovoked and threaten to beat them up. I made sure to keep a safe distance from Norman, and I was thankful that he never got to me.

Back in the day, parents didn't ask about their kids' social condition at school. They were mostly concerned about the grades you were getting. If the grades were good, then they assumed everything else was okay. Nowadays, parents need to ask questions and know what's going on with their kids. With bullying, social issues, depression, and various kinds of pressure that young kids face these days, parents must regularly have conversations with their kids to understand any challenges they may be facing in their personal lives.

✲ ✲ ✲

Every guy in our class was convinced he'd make it to the NBA one day. Basketball wasn't just a game to us; it was life. We played at school, in our backyards, and practically anywhere we could find a hoop. You were only considered a "main man" at school if you rocked white Converse all-stars—better known as "Chucks"—with colored shoelaces. But me? I only had PF Flyers, a knock-off of Converse. And that was a problem. I couldn't keep showing up on the court, slipping and sliding across the gym floor with my PF Flyers as if I was on skates!

Naturally, I decided I had to upgrade my style. I asked my mom to take me to Olympia Sporting Goods on Livernois and 7 Mile so I could get a pair of Converse. She obliged and was cooperative until she took one look at the $11.95 price tag and shut down fast.

"That's too much for a pair of gym shoes!" she said. "That's money for a week's worth of food, boy."

But I wasn't giving up. I got myself a paper route, saved up, and finally bought my first pair of Chuck Taylors. Not long after, I made the junior varsity team at Hampton—the Hampton Hawks. It was my first organized basketball team, and I was beyond proud to wear that uniform. Though I didn't get much playing time because I wasn't tall enough, I didn't mind too much. I was just happy to sit on the bench, glowing in the team uniform, suited up with my teammates.

I tried my hand at many sports during the years I spent in Hampton Junior High. Still, something kept drawing me back to music. Have you ever been preoccupied with the thought that you were meant to do something with your life? And no matter how you try to get away, destiny always finds a way to drag you back to that thing? That was how I felt about music. It always felt like a destiny that kept calling out to me. I was convinced I was supposed to be a singer or play an instrument.

I sometimes thought that maybe if I applied myself and practiced enough, I could become a master of music.

It was years later that I realized this strong desire had been planted in my heart for a reason. God was the one drawing me to music, but it would take some work to discover and develop my craft. As a young boy, I didn't have the discipline to make myself practice, and this is where parents are needed to pull that gift out of their child. My mother wanted me to play an instrument, and though she took the pains to buy one for me and even hire a tutor, I needed her to take that extra step to ensure that I learned.

There were a couple of guys who played in a band in junior high. Randall Jacobs, a very good guitar player, Ronald Brock, who played bass, and Steve Bacon on drums. The three guys played the loudest rock music I had ever heard, and they quickly rose to fame, becoming the main attraction at our talent shows. Inspired by these three boys, I decided to enter the next talent show. I formed a group with Michael Harris, Dean Boyce, and Jeffery Dennis, three of my friends, and we practiced every day in my basement, rehearsing the Delfonics' classic *"La-La (Means...I Love You)."*

I enlisted the help of my two brothers, Andy and Reggie, who were now very good musicians in their own right, and they coached and rehearsed with us every day after school. Andy and Reggie made sure we sang the right notes, and they worked on our harmony. At the end, we had a good enough performance. We didn't get booed off the stage, but we didn't win the first prize either. This event was my last attempt at becoming a musician. The next year, I volunteered to be the MC of the talent show. Standing on the stage and introducing each act felt natural to me, and I immediately knew that this was what I wanted to do.

It was, however, difficult to let go of music completely. The sound of bands in our basement still shook the neighborhood whenever Reggie and his friends had their jam sessions. My mother also kept the music playing in the house through the old radio that never seemed to switch off except after midnight. I remember waking up in the fall of '72 to the familiar voice on the new radio station, 1400 WJLB, cheering me awake every morning with that high-pitched, cheerful call, "Get up! It's the Percolator!"

"Al Perkins!"

"Here's that sound from that voice you love!"

"It's Al Green, ya'll!" He would introduce the music seamlessly as the beat picks up. "Let's stay together."

Al Perkins would talk right up to half a second before Al Green's first vocals drift through the radio speakers with that smooth line, "I'm so in love with you..."

I was always so impressed by the way the DJs had mastered the timing to allow their voice to drift slowly into the first line of the artist's song.

I fondly remember how my mother would stop anything she was doing as the clock ticked towards noon. She would take a seat at the dining room table and listen to the radio. Her favorite show, "Inspiration Time," started at noon on WJLB. The presenter, Martha Jean "The Queen," a legendary radio personality, was one of the first black radio announcers in Memphis, TN. She first worked at WDAS for many years before relocating to Detroit to work for WJLB.

My mother never missed a day of this show, and it typically began with James Cleveland and his choir singing "Without a Song" as the background introduction to Queen's show.

She always dedicated that intro to "the sick and the shut-in" as she started a discussion. You could be sure that my mother would repeat every word of wisdom she picked up from that day's show until we knew exactly what Martha Jean the Queen said about the topic.

After I got home from school, a guy named Claude "The Big Soul Rocker" Young would be on the air for his afternoon drive shift. The Big Soul Rocker was energetic with a polished delivery that was always entertaining to listen to. You would also hear Claude doing many entertainment concerts and radio commercials for places like Henry's Cocktail Lounge, Phelps Lounge, and many more! His voice was my favorite when it came to announcing that we could see artists like "Tyrone Davis live at Henry's!" The way Claude used his dynamic voice and energy to get people excited about the artists coming to town inspired me. It's where I first developed the style I still use today when voicing concert spots—thanks to Claude "The Big Soul Rocker" Young!

After Claude was Donnie Simpson, better known as "The Love Bug." I could really relate to Donnie because he was 16 when he landed his first job on the radio in Detroit at 1400 WJLB. Donnie followed Claude for the evening shift at 6 p.m. and started his show off with a song by the Supremes called "Love Is Like an Itching in My Heart." As the drum beat of the song would start, Donnie would come on the air with excitement, saying, "It's 6 o'clock! And this is The Love Bug, Donnie Simpson!" Then the opening lyrics of the song would hit, *"The Love Bug done bit me...!"*

Quite honestly, Donnie was my favorite. His voice, his personality, and his intimate connection with the listeners were always intriguing to me. This was how I wanted to sound on the radio one day. Donnie always shared intimate stories about his life on the air—the love he had for his girlfriend who became his wife, Pam, and the most touching thing I have ever heard a jock do on the air: Donnie shared the birth of their first child, who he called "The Baby Bug," Donnie Jr. This was my idol on the air. Many days, I would find myself sitting in front of the radio as a teenager, imitating Donnie Simpson! I stayed glued to his show every night!

Because the radio often stayed on in our house all day, I didn't get to watch much TV. My mother's love for music was unmatched, and it was one of her few favorite things in the world. I remember back in the '70s when Al Green, The Temptations, and Gladys Knight came out with new LPs. My mother would send me to the record store to buy those records, and I would rush back home with the records secured in both hands. Then, my mom and siblings would sit around the stereo and listen to the newest releases. We would enjoy the evening breeze swaying through the living room, as the curtains danced in the open windows, and the voices of these great musicians carried through our souls.

    This was one of the greatest things about music back then. It brought the entire family together!

Things God spoke to me:

*"I'm giving you wisdom to accomplish everything I have put before you to do.
Continue to seek my instructions,
and you will know what to do and say in every situation.
Trust me, Gerald. You are my faithful servant.
Sometimes it may feel unsure, but you can trust me.
Enjoy this day I have created for you.
You know my voice."*

Chapter Four

Mumford High School

Nothing prepared me for high school, and I certainly didn't expect to create such a memorable adventure within the baby blue brick walls of Mumford High School. My saving grace was that I had several friends who also graduated from Hampton Junior High. Mumford High was a gigantic school with three floors as wide as soccer fields. My first day in school had me bumping shoulders with the throng of students who, like me, were finding their way through the floors, searching for their classrooms. Throughout my stay in high school, it was always a challenge rushing through the stairwells and finding my way from the first floor to my classroom on the top floor, just before the bell rang and the doors shut.

I had high hopes of being a star basketball player in my high school. Like most of my friends, I believed that it was at Mumford that my backyard basketball skills and hidden talent would finally be unearthed.

I was looking forward to joining the legendary Mumford Mustangs, a team that had several players with city-wide reputations like Dwight Darbins, Punchy Martin, Joe Jones, Herky Jerk, Darryl Bryant, and Kevin Moore. I was a former member of my junior high basketball team, and I was confident I could finally become recognized for something. I signed up for the tryouts and participated in the grueling practice sessions coordinated by the team coach, Dwight Jones. However, even before the final team roster was released, I knew I didn't stand a chance. I still hadn't grown at all! And for a sport where size was one of the most crucial qualifications, my 5'1 height was nowhere near what was required.

The tryouts were always packed with boys like me who wanted to be the next big basketball player, but at the end of the drills, Coach Jones released almost everyone who applied. He already knew who his players were, and most of us didn't stand a chance of making the JV or Varsity teams. It was at this point that the message finally became clear to me that basketball was not my calling. This realization motivated me to find out what I was supposed to do with my life. I was now in the 10th grade, and I had this burning desire to find my talent and find my own path in life.

In 1972, my father's skills and reputation had grown to the point where he started his own electrical contracting company. He named the new business McBride and Sons, with my brothers, Andy and David, now working as part of the company. Reggie had been clear about his musical calling since he was 15, and all he ever wanted to do was to play the bass. He had established himself as a musician, playing locally with different bands, building his brand as a professional bass player, and making money with his talent.

I will never forget late in 1972 when Reggie was recruited to play bass for The Dramatics, a group that was popular throughout Michigan. I remember the day when two members of the band, Ron Banks and Larry Demps, stopped by our house to ask my mother if she would allow

Reggie to go on tour with the group. My brother was in the 11th grade at the time, which meant he would have to quit school and go on the road for a year. To my teenage mind, this seemed like a brilliant idea, as I imagined my 16-year-old brother playing alongside one of the hottest singing groups of the 70s. But my mother wasn't too excited about the idea. She was concerned about his young age and what such exposure could do to his young mind, especially with him being around a bunch of grown men. Besides, Mom always wanted us to complete high school, and she explained her reservations and fears to Ron Banks and Larry Demps.

Ron Banks listened to my mother and made a personal promise to her that he would look after Reggie and ensure he was protected on the road.

When Mom reiterated that Reggie must complete his education, Ron Banks crossed his arms and looked intently into my mother's eyes.

"I promise you that Reggie will get his GED on the road," he told Mom. "Your son is important to the success of this band, and I will do everything within my power to make sure that he becomes a son you will be proud of."

My mother didn't have much to say after such a strong assurance from Ron Banks. She finally gave in, and Reggie went on to become The Dramatics' bass player.

We seldom saw Reggie afterwards. He went on several tours in different cities with The Dramatics, who were the opening act for James Brown's performances. As my brother later told us, James Brown approached him while they were on the road and asked, "How old are you?"

My brother answered that he was 16, and James immediately insisted that Reggie be allowed to go back home and complete his education. He assured Reggie that he could join the band on the tour after getting his GED. That said, Reggie returned home to study for the GED and, after a couple of months, earned his high school diploma. With his GED now completed, Reggie was allowed back on the road for the rest of the tour. I think this speaks volumes about Mr. Brown's integrity and attitude towards education.

Reggie's music career kept him on the road for two more years before he completed the tour with The Dramatics. He came home briefly and then spent another couple of years playing bass for Stevie Wonder. Once he had established himself as a renowned musician, Reggie moved to California and played for many other artists like Al Jarreau, Rare Earth, Bette Midler, and many other big names.

In the summer of 1973, my father received several big contracts for apartment buildings in Detroit. Though my brothers were fully engaged with the company, the massive electrical work on the ground was getting overwhelming for the team. They needed more hands, and my father recruited me to work for him on the projects. Typically, our day would start at 8:00 am sharp, with all the company employees meeting and charting a work plan for the day. My job was to go to each apartment that was still under construction with fresh drywall and install plugs. By the time noon rolled around, I would be covered with white drywall dust as I made my way to the lunch truck. In truth, nothing really excited me about this job except the lunch truck, which had the best sandwiches. I was also motivated by the pay I received at the end of the week. Besides the pay and the lunch, I had no enthusiasm whatsoever for this kind of work. Though I tried to enjoy it and give it my best shot, it didn't take long for me to realize that this also wasn't what I wanted to do in life. I was more fascinated by the summer basement parties that my sister and I organized for our neighborhood friends, who snuck in through the back door until the place was packed! I was always the DJ, supplying the music for these parties, and I found much joy blasting music until about 10 pm, when my mother would shout, "Party's over!" while banging on the basement door.

In 1974, during my sophomore year at Mumford, my mornings often started with the roar of a 1972 bright orange Dodge Dart right in front of our house as my friend, Lloyd Taylor, pulled up to pick me up. With me in the front seat beside Lloyd, the car's 8-track player would blast several music selections, including B.T. Express's "Do It 'Til You're Satisfied" all the way to school. Without fail, we'd speed down Curtis Boulevard at 60 miles per hour—more than double the speed limit, as we raced toward school. The sheer thrill of this dangerous adventure would make the hair on the back of our necks stand up, and the thought of it still sends a rush through my body today. One thing was certain—we were never late!

By this time, I had come to terms with the fact that basketball wasn't my calling, and my NBA dreams had faded away as I began thinking seriously about what I might be good at doing. Determined to get my answers before I finished high school, I became more intentional about choosing my classes for the semester. I selected Drama, Radio/TV, and Creative Writing, along with the mandatory Algebra II, Economics, and Gym. At first, the only reason I picked those electives was that they seemed fun and easy. But as the semester unfolded, I realized they were exactly where I needed to be.

Drama class was taught by Mr. Bob Curran, one of the most beloved teachers at Mumford. His class took place right on the auditorium stage, and from the moment I stepped onto it, something inside me clicked. He taught us everything from monologues to improvisation, and at the end of each semester, we were cast in the school play. Mr. Curran saw something in me that I had never even imagined was there. He believed in my talent, and his encouragement planted the first seed of confidence within me. Beyond being an incredible teacher, Mr. Curran had a side gig as the booth announcer for WXON Channel 20 in Detroit. I'd hear his smooth, commanding voice on TV, delivering the station's legal ID: "You're watching WXON Channel 20, Detroit." Every time I heard it, I thought, *"One day, that could be me."*

Mr. Curran's classes were a mix of structure and spontaneity as he often threw us into improvisation sessions without much notice, laughing heartily at our performances. The friendship our drama teacher displayed really made us comfortable on stage, gave us confidence, and pushed us to be better. Personally, Mr. Curran believed in me so much that he cast me in the lead role of our school play, *The Perfect Idiot*. No pun intended! We even modernized the script to fit our personalities, and when we finally performed it, the audience erupted in applause, giving us a standing ovation. That night, I discovered something new about myself. I could act!

Looking back, that experience was a defining moment. It wasn't just about performing; it was about someone believing in me. There are several instances when Mr. Curran would call me aside and say to me, "You can do this. You have what it takes." He even went as far as assuring me to pursue acting as a career, telling me, "You have what it takes to make it in this business." Those words, along with others I'd hear throughout my journey, shaped the path to where I am today. And through it all, my mother was always there for me, whether sitting proudly in the audience, beaming with joy, or offering words of encouragement to give me confidence. I quickly learned that there's nothing more powerful to a child than a parent's approval. If you have a child in your life, show up for them. Whether it's sports, the arts, or any other passion they pursue, be there, cheer them on, and let them know how proud you are.

Because of my success in drama, I was chosen to emcee Mumford's legendary talent shows. With past participants of this show going on to become incredible musicians and singers, including Earl Klugh, my brother Reggie McBride, The Clark Sisters, The Winans, and Fred Hammond, these talent shows were the events of the year. So, when I was selected to be the emcee, I was excited but also nervous. This was going to be my first time hosting, and I wanted to make a good impression. My first challenge was that I didn't have the right clothes for the occasion. Luckily, I could count on my oldest brother, Marvin, for help. Marvin and his wife, Francine, lived just a couple of blocks from school. I used to spend a lot of time at his place. Marvin himself was almost always out of the house hustling, so I mostly hung out with his wife, Francine.

Francine took charge of my wardrobe for the Mumford talent show. She went into Marvin's closet and picked out some of the sharpest outfits for me to wear that night. Being over two decades older than me, of course, Marvin's clothes were two sizes too big for me. Francine went to work on one of the outfits, and with the help of some safety pins here and a little tape there, she made the clothes look like a perfect fit on me. Still, she made sure to warn me to be very careful once I got on the stage.

As she looked me over and admired her work, Francine had a wry smile on her face. "Remember not to be too loose," she warned me. "You know you can only count on safety pins so much."

Thanks to Francine, I took to the stage with much swag the night of the show. Dressed in my brother's oversized clothes, I was very careful not to make too many outlandish moves that would make my pants fall down.

Francine was one of the most influential people in my life. She introduced me to the world of live music and entertainment, taking me to my first Motown Revue at the Fox Theatre when I was just 12. It was that night that I saw real legends—Gladys Knight, Stevie Wonder, The Four Tops, Marvin Gaye, Smokey Robinson and The Miracles, and, of course, The Temptations. She also took me to matinees at places like Henry's Cocktail Lounge, where I watched acts like Harold Melvin & The Blue Notes with Teddy Pendergrass, The Manhattans, The Dynamic Superiors, and The Stylistics. Francine always had the latest records, exposing me to a vast range of R&B music—knowledge that would serve me well later in life as a radio DJ.

A few hours before the talent show, I told Francine about my nerves. She looked at me and asked, "What are you afraid of?"

I tried to answer, but nothing came to me, so I said, "I don't know."

She smiled at me, as if I had just emphasized her point. And then, she told me quite frankly, "There is nothing to be afraid of. Just get out there and do it. Be yourself!"

Her words stuck with me, and I got the courage I needed to step onto the stage with confidence. Just like that evening, and on several occasions over the next few years, Francine continued to push me to become better, encouraging me to reach for bigger things, step out of my comfort zone, and give my best, even if I was afraid. She would continue to influence my life in the future, as she was always the person who pushed me to higher heights. Francine, Mr. Curran, and my mother, each in their own way, helped shape me into the person I would become. Their belief in me gave me the courage to believe in myself. And that, I've learned, is where success truly begins.

Once the talent show started, I was locked in. Determined to deliver excellent work, I forgot all about my nerves and doubts as I introduced the first act, a group of four brothers who were making their first appearance in front of the Mumford audience. As I introduced The Winans, I realized that my tone and inflection were a direct result of the training received from my radio broadcasting class. That education had more than prepared me for that moment and many more for decades to come.

That class was taught by Ms. Ward, an elderly English teacher who was a stickler for pronunciation, articulation, and good diction. The way a word was pronounced seemed more important to her than the technical part of radio. When you think about it, how could you be successful on the radio without good articulation and diction?

While I was a student in Ms. Ward's radio broadcasting class, I had the opportunity to do the weekly school announcements over the general P.A. system. This was a big deal to me as my voice was heard all around the school premises. I also had the opportunity to provide the lunchroom music with current R&B songs from the 1970s and a message for the student body. I remember one of my favorite songs to play that the lunchroom crowd loved was "We're a Winner" by the Impressions, which I still play on the radio to this day. That same year, I entered a citywide school contest for commercial scriptwriting and voice-overs, took second place in the Metro Detroit competition, and received a trophy that I still have as a reminder of what my high school, Mumford, told me I could be and do.

This led to an opportunity to become a Soul Teen Reporter representing Mumford on 1400 WJLB. This was no longer a P.A. system, but a real radio station! Finally, my dream was coming to pass right in front of my eyes, and I couldn't contain my excitement.

Once every week, I would catch the bus downtown to WJLB, which was located in the David Broderick Towers on Madison Avenue. Other high school students also came to the radio station from different parts of the city, including Cass Tech, Osborne, Cooley, Mackenzie, Henry Ford, and more. Each student teen reporter was given a chance to record their minute-long report on what was happening at their school, and the weekly recording session was handled by Donnie Simpson. As you might already know, Donnie Simpson later rose to fame as one of the most successful radio personalities in the world, with his radio career taking off in DC and being the host of BET's Video Soul. If you'll remember, Donnie was known in Detroit for his show, "The Love Bug," heard from 6 pm to 10 pm every day.

Our recordings took place in the production room of WJLB, where Donnie would record us on reel-to-reel tape recorders. He typically gave us only one take, so we had to come fully prepared with what we wanted to say. And if we made a mistake, it was fascinating for me to watch Donnie expertly edit the error with a grease pencil and razor blade on a reel-to-reel tape recorder. His dexterity with those trained hands and great radio production skills were a joy to watch. I honestly could have sat in the radio studio for hours just to enjoy watching him work his magic. I remember one day, I was in the studio while Donnie worked on a radio commercial for Badd Records. As I sat there watching him do the voice-over into the mic while reading over the edited music bed he had created on reel-to-reel, then hearing it all come together perfectly into a 60-second spot, I was blown away! This was the first time I really thought, "*This is what I want to do and the person I want to sound like!*"

A few weeks later, Donnie gave me a lifetime opportunity! He selected me with a few other students and allowed us to watch him as he did his radio show. I was always a big fan of the show, and I listened to him every day, but nothing compared to being right there in the studio and watching him do it live. I will never forget how my heart pounded with excitement and the joy that coursed through my entire being as I witnessed that surreal moment. After this one chance to watch Donnie at WJLB, I decided there was nothing I'd rather do with my life than to be on the radio.

I have often said that you never know who is watching you, and the inspiration you can be to someone out there. At the end, we are all mentors, so remember to always set a good example, especially to the young people who may be watching you.

Things God spoke to me:

"Gerald, this time with you is so precious.
I am so pleased with how you share who I am and how to find me.
I will fill your thoughts and mind with ideas for movies and books.
Trust me that I can supply all your needs.
There's a special anointing on you to do this.
Trust me, my son, trust me. Step out and don't be afraid.
This is the way I can use people.
As they spend time with me so that I can give them my instructions.
They must know my voice.
The more they spend time with me, the more they will know my voice.
I am ready to give you many stories to tell.
And yes, the world will see the anointing on you.
Trust me as I open the next door. Trust me and trust what I'm saying to you.
I need you to be an example of my goodness and a relationship with me."

Chapter Five

✝

Post-High School Years & Many Firsts

I had enjoyed cruising in Lloyd Taylor's Dodge Dart long enough for me to look forward to driving on my own. He allowed me to sit behind the steering wheel and pretend to take the car for a spin a few times, but I wanted more. I was 16, in my sophomore year of high school, when I decided to take the driver's training at Mumford and get my permit. The training obstacle course was shaped like a figure 8 and located right in front of the school, complete with street lights, stop signs, pylons, and parking spaces for parallel parking. The speed limit on this small driver's training course was only about 10 mph, and I completed the course as quickly as possible. After taking the test, I received my permit with the confidence of a Formula 1 driver, ready for my first opportunity to get behind the wheel. I had my eyes on my father's sky-blue 1971 Cadillac Coupe Deville, and I was waiting for the day I would get a chance to drive...*for real.*

Julie, my sister, was visiting her friend a few blocks away when she called home to tell our parents that she was ready to come home. The friend's house was within walking distance of our house, but it was snowy, so she needed my dad to come pick her up. I heard my mom passing the message to my dad, and I decided this was an opportunity to finally drive. My dad had already picked up the car keys when I stepped into the living room.

"I'll go pick her up," I told my parents.

They didn't respond at first. I felt they didn't understand what I meant, so I said it again.

"Let me pick her up with your car," I told my father, my eyes pleading yet confident. My mother shook her head slowly and turned to look at my dad. Both of their faces reflected their doubt.

"I'm not sure," Mom directed the words to my dad, sensing that he might want to agree to my request. "It is just a few blocks away. I'll be back in no time," I told my dad and proceeded to collect the car keys.

My father had always told us boys to man up and be brave, so I directed most of my appeals to him. Besides, it was his car, and he had the final say.

My father nodded slowly, and I knew that was it.

I was on my way out when I heard his voice calling after me, "Be careful! Come straight back home!"

I was so excited as I went out of the house, the car keys rolling around my index finger. The first thing I did was to pick up my friend, Kenny, who lived right across the street.

It was a cold day in January with snow drizzling down on the street and patches of ice covering the roads. But I didn't mind; I was just excited to be behind the wheel with Kenny sitting beside me on the passenger seat. We cruised the Cadillac, hovering around 30mph as we approached

Cherrylawn Street. Once the car turned onto the residential street, I noticed cars parked on both sides. I was beginning to slow the car down when suddenly, I hit a patch of ice. Things went from bad to worse as the car slid out of control across the icy road and the brakes locked. Now sliding freely across the street, I held on to the wheel as Kenny and I screamed for the car to stop.

The Cadillac swerved, skidded off the road onto a driveway, smashed into a parked car, and finally landed on the front porch of the house. Next thing I heard in the commotion was Kenny's voice yelling, "Back up! Back up!"

His first thought was to try and make an escape, and I quickly sprang into action.

I tried to move the car and make a run for it. However, as I tried to back up, I stepped on the gas, but the Cadillac refused to move an inch. The wheels were spinning, but since we were stuck in the ice and snow on the front lawn, there was no friction to move the car.

"Get out of the car!" I heard the loud voice of a man and knew immediately that we were done for.

The owner of the house ran out onto the front porch and kept yelling for us to get out of the car. As I opened the door, the man grabbed me by the collar and dragged me out of the driver's seat.

"You were trying to get away, weren't you?!" The man was livid, his face red with anger.

I stumbled out of the car and stood there before the man in silence. I was shaking both from the cold and fear. I had never been so afraid in my life!

Still holding my collar, the man pulled me inside his house and made me call my parents. Of course, my dad was furious. He left the house in anger and walked over to Cherrylawn Street until he found the man's house.

My dad apologized profusely to the man and offered to cover all the damages, both on the house and the car. The entire front of my dad's Cadillac was also ruined, with thousands of dollars in damage. My father didn't have insurance on the car, so his much cherished Cadillac had to sit in the garage for a long time. Anytime I saw the damaged car, it served as a reminder of my reckless driving. The guilt and regret caused me a lot of pain and strained my relationship with Dad for years.

* * *

At the end of the school year in June 1975, my classmates and I went on a car-hopping spree in what was called "Senior Swing-out Day." It was a day set aside to cruising in cars and riding around all day, blasting the horns in celebration of our final days of high school. Huddled together in cars lined one after the other, we went around the city singing wildly and cruising to our class song, Earth, Wind & Fire's "Devotion."

On most days, we would end up at someone's basement, partying all night to some of the popular music of the moment. The Isley Brothers' 1975 LP, *The Heat Is On*, was enough to keep a party going all night. I loved the LP particularly because of the song arrangement. On one side of the LP were three fast songs everyone could dance to: "Fight the Power," followed by "The Heat is on," and then "Hope You Feel Better, Love." After jumping around the dance floor as we moved our bodies in rhythm with the fast songs until we were covered in sweat, we would flip the LP over, turn the lights down, and grab a partner as we slow-danced to "For the Love of You," "Make Me Say It Again, Girl," and "Sensuality."

A few weeks later, after the graduation parties and celebrations had come to an end, I was left to think about my future. I graduated from high school and had a clear direction of what I wanted to do in life. I was certain that my future belonged on the radio. *But how would I get my foot through the door?*

In the summer of 1975, an opportunity opened up for my brother, Marvin, to purchase a nightclub that had partially burned down, called The Burning Spear. The nightclub was located at the corner of Puritan and Santa Rosa, and the previous owners decided to sell after the fire. Marvin paid for the nightclub and hired me and some of my friends to help with the renovations. He also consulted with my dad on the redesign and reconstruction, as we spent long summer days and nights working on rebuilding the portions of the nightclub that had been destroyed in the fire.

After a few weeks, we completed the job, and the reopening of the nightclub was well-publicized. I was looking forward to becoming the house DJ in my brother's brand-new nightclub, but Marvin had other plans. He paid my friends and me our wages and let us go.

The club was an overwhelming success with a packed house in the discotheque every night. Business was so good that after a couple of weeks, Marvin decided to hire me as a dishwasher and porter for the bar section of the club in the evenings. He also hired my mother to work as a cook for the businessmen who were served at lunchtime. My work shift was split between night and daytime to help out wherever needed.

The discotheque was usually empty in the early hours of the day, and I took this opportunity to sneak into the DJ booth and work on the turntables.

"This is Brother Gerald live from the Burning Spear!" I would say into the mic, pretending that I was speaking to a room full of people. With my voice imitating Donnie Simpson's as best as I could, I would go on to say, "Here's Earth, Wind & Fire with their hit song, 'Keep Your Head to the Sky'."

I repeated this intro for days, improving my bass and working on my swagger in front of the microphone as I worked the turntables like an expert. Between washing dishes and stocking the bar, I snuck into the DJ booth and entertained an empty room every chance I got!

There were a few times when Marvin came in early and caught me in the DJ booth pushing the turntables. Furious, he would scream at me to get back to work.

"Didn't I tell you to stay out of that DJ booth?!" He would scream from the entrance. "Turn that thing off and get back to washing those dishes!"

* * *

One evening, the nightclub was open, and the bar was filled with people who were ready to party. However, when it was time to start dancing, Marvin and his staff realized that the DJ was nowhere to be found. He called to say he had been stopped for a traffic ticket and wouldn't be able to make it to the club that night. The entire staff began to panic, growing more agitated and on the verge of a crisis. I was in the back washing dishes in the kitchen when I heard what was going on. And then, Marvin walked up to me and made me the offer.

"I need you to be the DJ," he instructed, panicking. "You can do it, can't you?"

I didn't need further convincing. I cleaned my hands and hurriedly followed Marvin out of the kitchen. I knew my way around the DJ booth already and was on the turntables within a minute. *This is my big break, and I will make the best of it!*

I knew my way around the music catalogue and threw on "Jam Dazz" by Brick. The crowd was already itching to hear some music, so it was a perfect jam to get the crowd going.

As was the custom, the first thing a DJ does is to introduce himself and the music. So, I drew towards the mic and said my name.

"This is Brother Gerald." Those four words sounded perfect to my ears. "Welcome to the fabulous Burning Spear!"

I was grinning from ear to ear as I started spinning the turntables as the speakers boomed to the beat of Brick's hit, "Jam Dazz."

The audience responded with a rumble, and then I could hear them say, "Yeah! Yeah...!" as people stood up from their seats, ready to party. The fellas rushed to find the ladies, and the dance floor soon became packed with people.

Right then and there, I felt like I had arrived. I had finally found my place in the world, and there was no feeling that could compare to the sense of utter joy that filled me.

"This is where I am supposed to be!"

As the music changed and the people roared to the song I played for them, I looked around and saw Marvin standing at the back, just beside the entrance. He was looking at me, and his face broke into a proud smile as our eyes met. He didn't need to utter one word for me to understand that I had just secured a new job and earned his respect.

I became the full-time house DJ for Burning Spear after that first night, and when the regular DJ returned, there was no need to engage him anymore. The people had a great time with me, and that was all that mattered to Marvin. I worked as the house DJ seven days a week and made 35 dollars per night, which was good pay in 1976. A few weeks later, Marvin changed the marquees to add my name to the sign:

*"Disco Tonight
With Your DJ, Brother Gerald,
Playing The Music."*

The nightclub was known to be a place frequented by drug dealers, pimps, and all kinds of hustlers, and it was certainly not the best environment for a young man like myself. Yet, despite my ignorance at that time, I find it amazing that God's grace and mercy surrounded and protected me from these vices. Though I didn't know God then like I do now, He had a plan for my life even when I didn't realize it.

Working in the nightclub was an adventure I really enjoyed, but I didn't forget that my ultimate dream was to be on the radio someday.

I decided I needed a degree in Broadcasting to get myself on this path. I enrolled in Spec Howard's School of Broadcasting, a nearby trade school. It took a single visit to Spec Howard for me to know I had made the right decision. The classes were very hands-on as we worked with simulated radio stations that broadcast through the entire building.

Thank God I was able to pay my way through school with the $35 a night I made from the Burning Spear.

It was in this school that I met Dick Kernan. His job as the Head of Placement was to make sure the students secured a job at a radio station upon graduation. One day, I was walking down the hallway after my shift on the radio, when I met Dick.

"Are you the one who was just on the air?" he asked.

I said yes with a big smile.

He seemed pleased to meet me and gave me a firm handshake. "I had to come out of the office to identify who that voice was on the air. Sounds like you could have a great future in this business," he added before walking away. This brief conversation with Dick meant a lot to me, and I was motivated to keep going on my journey to become a professional in the broadcasting business.

After graduation from Spec Howard, we all received diplomas. We also got our résumés and air-check demo tapes to send with our applications to radio stations. I always carried around an old, small reel-to-reel tape recorder that played my air-check demo tape everywhere I went and to anybody who would listen to it. My girlfriend at the time probably heard that demo tape at least a thousand times!

Things God spoke to me:

*"Come to me, Gerald. Nothing has changed.
You are still my faithful son.
Forgive, for I have forgiven you.
My instructions are also available for you,
so that when you make a mistake, you will know to correct it.
I know you will make a few mistakes.
Trust me, Gerald, and trust my love for you.
You know my voice.
Gerald, I need you to be an example of my forgiveness and goodness and mercy."*

Chapter Six

My Radio Journey

Disco came onto the music scene in 1977, with different genres of music gaining popularity. Disco halls became the rave of the moment, and several bars sprang up in the city. With the growing competition, the crowd at The Burning Spear dwindled drastically, and Marvin started exploring other music styles to stay in business.

We parted ways as I was now concentrating on going into radio full-time and couldn't afford to spend my nights in the bar. In the meantime, I got a job as a stockperson at Beckwith Evans, a carpet company on Livernois in Detroit. My main duty at the job was to receive the carpets when they were delivered and stock them in the store. I also helped to keep the store clean.

Though this kind of job was not what I was expecting after graduating from broadcasting school, I remained hopeful. Dick Kernan had personally promised to get me an interview with some radio stations. Six months went by, and Dick still couldn't secure a placement for me; no radio station seemed to be interested. I continued working at Beckwith Evans, and the management acknowledged my hard work by allowing me to do some part-time sales work. This new role increased my weekly salary to $350. With this new pay, I bought my first car, a 1977 Pontiac Sunbird.

Despite a comfortable life at my parents' house, with no expenses beyond my car payment, my drive to pursue a career in radio never waned. I decided to send my demo tapes out myself, and I received a few interview requests, but still no radio job. Finally, I got a call from Dick Kernan.

"Hey, Gerald," he said. "I have a program director who heard your tape and likes it."

I was elated to hear this great news.

"He has a part-time opening at a radio station in Flint called WAMM." Dick asked, "Would you be interested in this opportunity?"

"Are you kidding?" I replied, unable to contain my joy. "Of course! Yes!"

Dick explained that the job was a Saturday afternoon shift from 3 pm - 6 pm. I called the program director, Greg Jones, and he asked if I could come to the radio station in Flint for orientation.

His plan was to have me sit in with one of their radio DJs from Monday to Friday to learn the format and the board before my Saturday debut shift. However, I wanted to do the right thing with my employer, Beckwith Evans. Although the notice was short, my boss knew it was my dream to be on the radio. When I told him about the opportunity, he gave me the approval to leave the carpet store for my trip to Flint for that week.

That following Monday, I sat in the booth and watched the announcer who was on the afternoon drive shift. Back then, the radio boards had several knobs and switches, with turntables that were barely within reach. As I sat there and watched day after day, I felt I had everything figured out, and I enjoyed just sitting there and learning from the experts.

Once Saturday came, it was my turn. This was the opportunity I had waited for all my life — and now, I was finally here. It was my moment, my destiny. All my preparation and choices led to this one day! I'll never forget the feeling I had as I stood in the studio, and the DJ on the previous shift concluded his session.

"That's it for me!" He said cheerfully into the mic. "And up next, our brand new DJ, Gerald McBride!"

When I heard him say my name, the adrenaline kicked in and brought a lot of nervousness and anxiety with it. I held my breath and calmed myself. As I sat down in the chair with the mic in front of me, the knobs and controls all started to look very confusing. I forgot everything I learned as my palms became sweaty. I was beginning to panic. I tried my best to hold it all together and to remind myself of what I had learned throughout the week, but my memory suddenly grew very foggy.

As the outro record began to fade, my first intro record on the turntable was cued up and ready to play. I put on my headphones, ready to say my first words on the radio.

The plan was to call out the letters of the station ID, *W-A-M-M-F-L-I-N-T*. However, what happened next was entirely different. As the outro record faded, I reached for the turntable to start my first song and hit the arm of the turntable across the 45 record.

What I heard next was the screeching noise of distortion that went across the airwaves. In a bid to salvage the moment, I opened up the mic to speak. But I had totally forgotten about the station ID I was supposed to give according to the director's instructions.

The program director ran into the studio and yelled at me. "What are you doing?!" Mr. Greg Jones was absolutely fuming.

I didn't know how to explain or what to say.

"Get out of here!" the director commanded. "You are fired!"

I heard those words as if they were daggers to my heart. My lifelong dream of being on the air had ended before it began. I had blown my chance right then and there before I could even say my first words on the radio.

Now that I look back on those days, I realize that where there is a destiny, God will reveal it regardless of the obstacles or setbacks. I went back to working my regular job at the carpet store, thinking I had blown my one shot at getting on the radio. *I will now be stuck here forever as the clean-up guy at this carpet store.*

Throughout the next few weeks, I lived in sadness and regret. I was both embarrassed by what had happened and frustrated that my dream had gone up in smoke. Truly, it was one of the lowest points in my life.

Two months later, just when I thought there was no way to get my radio career back on track, I received a call from the assistant program director at WAMM, John Tatum.

"Hello Gerald," he said. "This is John from WAMM in Flint."

"Hey John," I replied, surprised to hear from him. We had only met a few times during my one week of orientation and training.

He sounded pleased as he spoke with me. "I had a talk with Greg and told him that what happened was only a mistake," he began. "I explained that it was your first time on the air, and that you were probably pretty nervous."

I didn't respond just yet, as I was still lost for words.

John Tatum continued. "I thought we should give you another chance. Would you be interested in coming back up this weekend and giving it another try?"

It felt as if a miracle had happened! "Of course!" I jumped at the chance. "I will be there!"

I arrived at the station early that Saturday afternoon, and I was ready. As soon as the DJ from the previous shift introduced me, I quickly shifted gears and went to work. This time, I impressed both Greg Jones and John Tatum and was grateful to them for the second chance. They complimented my performance, and I was invited back for my Saturday afternoon shift the following week. And as they say...the rest is history!

I am a living testimony that God is a God of second chances, and not just second chances, but hundreds and thousands as I would learn throughout my life. Being on air meant everything to me. There is no feeling like knowing that you are exactly where you are supposed to be in life, living your dream. Throughout the week, while I worked at the carpet store, I would start counting down the days to the weekend, rehearsing my radio talk during the breaks between music.

Six months flew by as I became more and more comfortable on the airwaves. It was a thrill to talk to people on the request line, introducing songs while running a tight board and following the format. By this time, I had grown to know Greg Jones better, and he would always tell me how much he liked my sound on the air. He even hinted that it would offer me a chance to increase my airtime.

Shortly after my conversation with Greg, the daily midday DJ, Jay Allen, who was also working a full-time job at a nearby plant, decided he wanted to work only on weekends. His normal radio slot came on from 10 am to 3 pm every day except Sunday, but Jay Allen wanted to focus on his job at the plant. The program director asked if I wanted to take this slot, and I jumped at the opportunity. The radio offered to pay me $141.00 every two weeks, but that meant that I had to quit the carpet store. *How was I going to live on $141.00 every two weeks?!* It didn't matter that I was making far less than I made at the store. Deep in my heart, I knew this was my opportunity to work on the radio full-time, so I took the job without hesitation.

I moved to Flint with limited funds and shared an apartment at the Sunrise Apartment Complex with Floyd Little, a DJ who worked the afternoon shift. The rent was $240.00 a month for the two-bedroom apartment, and it seemed reasonable to split the rent out of my $141.00 bi-weekly salary. This was the first time I would live away from my parents, and the only thing I owned was the car.

After a few months, paying the car note for my fancy 1977 Pontiac Sunbird, became an issue. I fell behind on the payments, and became frustrated dealing with unceasing threatening phone calls from the bill collector. One day, as I stepped out of my apartment to jump in my ride, I noticed that my car was not in the parking lot. In a panic, I immediately called the police to report the car stolen. Next, I called the bill collector to file a formal report that the car had been stolen. I was, however, left in utter shock by their response. I was told that the company had repossessed the car and that the entire balance owed on the car would have to be paid up in full before I could get the car back. Of course, with my limited income, this was out of the question.

Without the car, traveling to the station on the other side of town became a real challenge. Back then, hitchhiking was safe enough, and I would stand on the road and get rides into town. To make sure I got picked up quickly, I would grab a few books and pretend I was going to school. So, there I was every day, standing along Flushing Road with my books in hand and my thumb stretched out. And soon enough, a car would stop, with the heart to help a student get to school early.

"Where are you headed?" The driver would roll down the window and ask.

"Mott College," I would reply.

"Right," the driver would beckon to me. "Hop in!"

Mott College was just a block away from the radio station, so it was an efficient strategy.

Across the street from the radio station was a small party store where we would always stop in before or after our shifts to grab sandwiches and snacks. With us going there almost every day, I got to know the owner, Pete, pretty well. I would share with Pete some of my financial struggles, and one day, he offered me a business opportunity to make a little extra money.

While I was in the store one day, Pete called me to the back and said, "Hey, Gerald, come here. I want to show you something." As I followed him to the back, he pulled out a big black Hefty garbage bag. He opened up the bag and said, "Take a look inside." As I look in the garbage bag, it's halfway filled with marijuana! WOW! I had never seen that much weed before. In my past, I may have smoked a few joints from time to time. Hanging out with all my friends, that is what we did most of the time, with maybe an ounce of weed at the most, but I had never seen this much weed!

Peter explained, "What you see right here is a pound of weed. I'll make a deal with you. If you can sell all of this weed, you can make some money. The pound of weed is four hundred dollars, but if you sell it all, you can make eight hundred dollars. All I need is my four hundred dollars back." To me, this seemed like a great business opportunity, and I really needed the money. I took Pete up on his offer and took the weed back to my apartment.

Each day after a couple of pick-up basketball games at the Sunrise Apartments, I would invite a few friends I met on the court over to the apartment to smoke a couple of joints with them and try to sell them a bag or two. Unfortunately, after a couple of months and a few smoking parties, I found the weed to be all gone, and, thanks to poor mismanagement, the profit I was supposed to make was also gone. For weeks, I would avoid going to the store, knowing that Pete would eventually ask about his weed or the money. Finally, I had to tell him. When asked, I told him the truth: I mismanaged the money and smoked all the weed. He was furious and demanded that I pay him back. I made a promise to pay him back, but never did. Needless to say, I never went into the store again. Also, I learned I could never be a drug dealer who smoked his own product.

Being on the air was a lot of fun, but after every shift, there was production work to complete. Production was the bread and butter of the station, as it included the commercial ads that ran on air. Each DJ had to perform these duties in the production room equipped with two-track reel-to-reel tape recorders, two-track cart machines, one microphone, a turntable, and a small mixing board. There were also pre-produced commercials on reel-to-reel from production houses that needed to be transferred onto the two-track carts before they were played on air. Then there were scripts that needed to be read and recorded by each one of us.

Most of the radio clients at WAMM were local advertisers and businesses like Karen's Carpets, Shorthorn Meats, Piece of the Rock Night Club, and many other small companies. Being heard live on air was great, but the real work was off the air when you went into the production room, checked your basket, and found that you had several commercials to produce, sometimes for several hours.

WAMM taught me several things that became quite important throughout my career. Besides the work ethic I built while working in the production room, I also learned financial management from making $141.00 every two weeks. Remarkably, I also explored my production, voice-overs, and script writing skills. Clients began to notice my unique voice and name after I produced commercials for a wide range of products and events. Soon, I was specifically requested to be the voice for their ads. Discovering my gift for producing commercial ads served as another confirmation of my career in radio production.

In my first year on the radio, Deanne, my girlfriend, moved in with me and became pregnant. I remember being so scared, wondering how we were going to make it on my meager $141.00, which was hardly enough to support myself. It was impossible to raise a family on that income. But I was willing to take on this responsibility as I welcomed the opportunity to become a father. Once again, here comes God to the rescue.

Six months into the pregnancy, another job would be offered to me at another brand-new Flint radio station called WDZZ. The offer was for twice as much money with insurance benefits that were right on time for the arrival of my son, whom I would name Jerald Jaz McBride. My roommate Floyd moved out to make room as Deanne and I started our family in the small two-bedroom apartment.

Now that I reflect back on this, I realize that 20 is very young to start a family and take on this huge responsibility. But even though I was so unsure, I knew I had to step up to take care of my son. Deanne and I got married, and life took on a new meaning and a new challenge, making my decisions and my career more crucial. It wasn't just about me anymore. I had to take things more seriously because others were counting on me.

Even to this day, I still see myself stepping out into the unknown, not knowing what the future may hold. Fatherhood seemed to be that way. But when my son was born, it was one of the most loving and exciting days of my life. Here I was at the young age of 20, bringing a person into this world who could continue my legacy. Jaz being born into this world was a bundle of joy. I remember looking at him in his crib many times when he was an infant and thinking, "Wow! This is my son!" Having a child at this young age helped me grow as a person. But I still had a lot of growing to do and a lot to learn.

Things God spoke to me:

Gerald, I have heard your request.
You asked me to get involved with every detail of
your life.
So you can continue to please me and do what honors me.
Know that I have heard you.
I am pleased with you, Gerald.
A hedge of protection is around you and your family.
Trust me, Gerald, as I will never leave you or
forsake you.
Trust me as I guide you each and every step.
Trust me as I lead you into the promised land.
And then, people will see what I have done in your life,
and they will want it.
You will tell them that it is I who provides the increase.
It is I who wants a relationship with them for the best in
their lives.
It works. They just need to come to me.
My arms are open wide to receive and love them.

Chapter Seven

THE
BIG
BREAKS

WDZZ was founded by Vernon Merritt in 1979 as the Flint area's first FM station to target African-American audiences, playing a mixture of disco music and jazz, which eventually evolved into mainstream urban contemporary. It is believed that the call letters were a tribute to the song "Dazz" by the group Brick. "Dazz" was an amalgamation of "disco" and "jazz."

Before 92.7 signed on, WAMM 1420 (now WFLT) served as Flint's rhythm & blues station, with its only competition being Saginaw's WWWS, which did not provide a clear signal over much of the Flint area.

The station brought in a brand-new staff of air talent. Don Wiggins was program director and also hosted mornings from 6 am to 10 am; Bill Meyers conducted the midday; Curtis "Sly" Foxx had the afternoon shift; and Jason St. Clair had the evenings. Then yours truly was on from 10 pm to 2 am, followed by Cleodia Myles from 2 am to 6 am.

I was so excited to be part of this brand-new station, high atop the Genesee Towers in downtown Flint, with a beautiful view of the city. WDZZ had an immediate impact. The station debuted at number one in the Arbitron ratings in its first full ratings period with a share of over 11%. This was the spring of 1980, when Flint was measured by Arbitron only once per year. WAMM never recovered and soon flipped formats to the Music of Your Life as WFLT, eventually settling into the urban gospel format it has today.

Since my shift was at night, I spent the day at home with my wife and son. I was getting ready for my shift one day when I decided to review some newly released songs. I saw a new LP with the title *Gap Band III* written across the cover and a picture of three brothers wearing cowboy hats. As I dropped the needle on the record, the sound of an engine revving up, followed by screeching tires, filled the air as the unforgettable beat of the song "Burn Rubber" kicked in, with that unmistakable drum beat and a groove that would make anybody want to dance.

As the song played, my son Jaz staggered into the room on his little feet and started dancing. I will never forget the picture of seeing my one-year-old boy dancing to the beat of the lively music. And from that day forward, anytime I put this song on, Jaz would drop whatever he was doing, run into the room, stand in front of the stereo, and start dancing.

Jaz was always full of energy, and we had our hands full. I had a row of LPs stacked along the wall of the apartment, and Jaz would climb to the top as if it were a playground. As soon as I took him down off the stack, he would go right back and climb it all over again until this became a sort of game between the two of us.

On my 10 pm to 2 am night shift, the songs I played were mostly slow jams. One of my favorite songs to play on the show was "Yearning for Your Love" from the same *Gap Band III* LP. This nighttime slot gave me an opportunity to develop my smooth, quiet storm sound on the radio. I never thought my voice fit the "hype jock" radio style, but the tempo of the night shift seemed to fit my personality perfectly. To me, being on at night felt more intimate with the listeners. Other daytime shifts seemed like background music while people were at work, busy with chores, or getting in and out of the car. But at night, you would have more of their undivided attention. It was a chance to really connect with the audience.

From this shift, I learned not to think of speaking to a crowd, but to focus on one person, while still keeping in mind who the core audience is. Of course, at night when you're on the radio and you're playing mostly love songs, the majority of your audience is going to be ladies. So that is who I tried to appeal to. Don't get me wrong — guys love the music too; they just won't admit it like ladies do! Some of the most popular shows on R&B radio were the slow jam nighttime shows, like the "Quiet Storm" that originated in D.C., hosted by a jock by the name of Melvin Linsey, Vaughn Harper, who hosted the Quiet Storm in New York, and Alan Allman, who did Pillow Talk in Detroit, just to name a few. All of these shows had a history of extremely high ratings for nighttime radio.

As the months went by, the station was now generating adequate revenue, and all of the on-air DJs were treated like superstars in the community, being invited to host celebrity basketball games, make local appearances, and provide endorsements for various causes. During this time, I would also get promoted to music director in addition to my nighttime shift. The music director's role is to receive music from record companies, review it, and determine what's right for the station. These decisions aren't only up to the music director. Most of the time, it's the program director who makes the ultimate decisions for the station's playlist. Usually, it's the music director who makes strong recommendations to the program director, so it becomes a team effort.

Music directors are also responsible for meeting with the record representatives as they bring the product to the station to lobby for airplay. So once a week, I would meet with several promoters who brought a handful of records they felt were hits for the station. As I remember, most of the songs were okay and never got any airplay, but every now and then, they would introduce a song that had what we call "it," which was that hit song that would get high rotation on the station's playlist.

I recall once, during a record promoter meeting day, I had an appointment with a local promoter named Gordon Alderson. Gordon worked for Capitol Records and showed up with a handful of records for me to listen to. Every song we put on seemed to lack the sound I thought was hit-worthy. As Gordon sat in front of my desk, he made himself comfortable by putting his big cowboy boots on it and asked, "So Gerald, when are you going to play my record?" Gordon had this serious look on his face as I looked at the bottom of his size 12 cowboy boots. Honestly, his tone and look became a little intimidating. At that moment, I thought of the stories of payola and how DJs got into serious trouble and even had their lives threatened if they didn't play songs for the record company. How serious was this guy? Or was he just trying to scare me, knowing that this was my first MD job?

There was one record he was really trying to push. I had listened to the song several times, but I didn't think it would fit our musical flow or have the sound to make it a lasting hit. Gordon used his research to show me that the song was doing well on other stations across the country, but I wasn't buying it. I refused to give in to playing the record or sharing it with Don, the program director. Weeks later, I would find out I was wrong as the song climbed the charts to number one, and we had no choice but to play the record. The song was Yarbrough and Peoples' "Don't Stop the Music," a classic R&B song that still gets airplay to this very day! This proves that some major hits are unpredictable, and you have to let the public decide if it's going to be a hit.

Even though I held two positions at the radio station, I would never forget what I enjoyed most: radio production. The whole process of sometimes writing copy, voicing it, and finding the right background music for each spot was always especially fascinating.

One of my early influences at WDZZ was Don Wiggins, the program director. Don had a real talent for voicing radio spots. His legendary voice on the advert for Olla Mills Fish and Shrimp, a local restaurant, would make your mouth water. It was Don who taught me that voicing was more than the pronunciation of words and the pitch of voice; it was about transmitting the right emotion, feeling, and inflection into every word. When Don spoke about the meals offered at Olla Mills, you could feel the sensation of the dishes and imagine yourself biting into the delicious seafood. I picked up a lot of good pointers from Don that I apply to my style to this day.

After a couple of years at WDZZ in Flint, Deanne received a call from her cousin Jan, who was dating Brent Wilson, the program director at WLBS, a Detroit radio station. There was an opening for the overnight slot at WLBS, and Jan thought it could be a great opportunity for me. I didn't hesitate, I applied immediately, and with Brent's recommendation, I was hired for the overnight shift, which ran from midnight to 6 am. The pay was $275 a week, and at the time, this felt like a fortune!

WLBS was a stunning station located in Mt. Clemens, about 30 minutes outside Detroit. Unlike WDZZ and WAMM in Flint, which had a more grassroots feel, WLBS was the sister station of the legendary WBLS in New York and had brand-new, state-of-the-art equipment. Though the disco era had begun to fade by 1981, the station still rode the wave of its sophisticated sound, featuring smooth, polished radio personalities like Brent Wilson, Pat Edwards, James Brian Sucilliano, and Terri McCormick. It was the perfect fit for my style, especially for a late-night shift.

For the first few weeks, I commuted from Flint to Mt. Clemens, but eventually, I moved my family to an apartment just five minutes from the station. Moving day was grueling. My friends and I spent the entire day hauling our things from Flint, and by the time evening rolled around, exhaustion hit me like a brick. But there was no time to rest—I had to be on the air at midnight. By the start of my shift, I was absolutely exhausted, and I had to keep pouring myself cups of strong coffee to power through. But around 4:00 am, fatigue finally got the best of me. To brush off sleepiness, I decided a quick five-minute nap couldn't hurt. My plan was simple: find a long song—something that would buy me a little time—lie my head down, and recharge for a moment. I chose an eight-minute track by Kleer, "You Better Get Tough." The irony of this song title was lost on me at the time. At exactly 4:15 am, I hit play, rested my head on the console, and closed my eyes just for a moment.

I woke back up at 5:45 am.

Panic set in instantly. Back then, when the song on a record ended, the needle would keep bumping against the label at the center—a loud, unmistakable sound for anyone who owned vinyl to know the song was over. It was this empty sound that echoed through the airwaves for over an hour. When I finally realized what had happened, the phone lines were ringing off the hook, the hotline was flashing non-stop, and the police were at the door! Everyone thought something terrible had happened. I had only been at WLBS for a month, and I was certain I had lost my job. But in an act of sheer mercy, Brent Wilson and the General Manager allowed me to keep my job. God's mercy covered me that day—yet again.

When I was working at WLBS, I made a bet with some coworkers that I would go skydiving. It was both funny and strange because at this point in my life, I had never even been on a plane. I registered for skydiving lessons, and after an entire day of receiving instructions, the moment of truth arrived. I stepped out the door of a small aircraft, hovering 5,000 feet in the air. My adrenaline surged, and my nerves rattled like never before! Fear gripped me, but despite the fear and anxiety, I let go and jumped.

The instant my parachute deployed, everything changed. I was no longer falling; I was gliding. What kept me on the right track was a radio attached to me, with a person guiding me as I drifted through the air. He would say, "Alright, McBride, pull the right toggle." "Now pull the Left toggle". Without this person's direction, no telling where I might have landed.

The world below stretched wide, and the air wrapped around me in a calm, almost surreal embrace. It was a smooth, breathtaking descent. This memory of drifting across open air always made me wonder what would happen if we trusted God the same way? What if we were tuned in to the right frequency on God's radio to get his instructions as we trust Him? What if we let it all go, knowing that with Him, we are safe? If we surrender completely, the journey could be smoother than we ever imagined. Whatever fear you're holding onto today—release it. Trust Him. His plan is perfect.

Not long after my skydiving adventure, I was moved to the 10 pm to 2 am shift, which was fairly better than my previous shift. However, this promotion came with an intimidating challenge. My competition on the same time slot at our rival radio station, 107.5 WGPR, was none other than Electrifying Mojo.

Mojo was a legend. He captivated Detroit night after night for years, even before I started my career. He is recognized for having introduced many artists into the Detroit radio market, including Prince, Parliament-Funkadelic, The B-52's, and Kraftwerk, and was occasionally thanked on-air by the artists for his support of their work. Prince granted Mojo an exclusive telephone interview during an era when Prince rarely, if ever, granted interviews. He had a unique sound and style that kept listeners glued to their radios. I grew up listening to him, admiring his mastery of the theater of the mind. There were some nights when I wondered if anyone was tuning in to my show at all, knowing Mojo dominated the airwaves.

Then, one night, as I was answering the request line, something unbelievable happened.

I picked up the phone line and said, "WLBS, who's on the line?"

The next thing I heard was, "Hey, man, it's Mojo."

I was confused for a moment and felt it was a prank. Then, I froze as I realized it was really Mojo calling *me*. My excitement shot through the roof.

"Mojo! What's up, man? Wow! I've been a fan of yours for years! I listen to you every night on my way to the station! You are the greatest!" I kept going, singing his praises, telling him how much I admired his work.

What I didn't realize at that moment was that I wasn't just talking to Mojo. I was talking to Mojo live on his station, WGPR, over the airwaves. I had just hyped up my biggest competition on his show in the presence of his massive audience. It was a rookie mistake, one that did not sit well with WLBS management. They were beyond disappointed that I could fall for a trick like that. Not only had I embarrassed myself, but the station as well. It was enough to cost me my job, but fortunately, I was allowed to stay on with a warning to watch out for calls from the competition, especially from Electrifying Mojo! Since then, Mojo and I have become good friends and often laugh about that night on the radio.

During my first year at WLBS, I focused on sharpening my production and voice-over skills. That dedication paid off when my voice caught the ears of two local promoters, Quinten Perry and Billy Sparks. They ran Taurus Productions, the largest concert promotion company in Metro Detroit, handling shows for legendary acts such as Earth, Wind & Fire, The Isley Brothers, Maze, Gladys Knight, and more. Billy Sparks and I worked closely together creating concert ad spots to promote upcoming shows, and soon, I became the official voice of Taurus Productions. My recording sessions would start after my shift ended at WLBS at 2 am and sometimes stretch until 7 am, just to complete a single commercial spot.

Back then, creating a 60-second concert ad was an art form that could take hours to produce. I did these commercial spots in WLBS' production room in the middle of the night before I went home in the morning. There was no digital editing, just reel-to-reel tape recorders and cart machines. First, I had to go through several songs to find the perfect clips from the featured artist's songs. Then, I'd record each clip onto the reel-to-reel. The next step was to mark the tape with a yellow grease pencil at the points where I wanted to cut the songs, then join them back-to-back with a smooth transition to create a cohesive music bed. Once the music bed was ready, I'd write the script. The format was typically short, with few words. It would go something like this:

> *This will be an amazing night of music with Jeffrey Osborne—live in concert!" (Song clip) Jeffrey Osborne! (Song clip) March 16th at the Masonic Temple! (Song clip) With special guest, Stephanie Mills! (Song clip) Don't miss Jeffrey Osborne and Stephanie Mills—be there! (Song clip)*

And every spot ended with the signature line: *"This is another Taurus Production!"*

While one tape recorder played back the 60-second music bed, another tape recorder would be in record mode, simultaneously recording my voice over the music. I layered everything together manually to create the commercial. It was time-consuming work, but it was worth it. I was paid $50 per spot—a much-needed blessing on top of my $275-a-week salary.

Taurus Productions gave me a new level of recognition in Detroit. I was now voicing two to three spots a week, and this served as a steady stream of extra income that arrived right on time as Deanne and I found out we were expecting our second child—our daughter, Brandy Lynn.

Years before Brandy was born, I had a dream that was quite vivid. In the dream, my daughter was about seven years old, with fair skin, dressed in a beautiful white dress with big red ribbons in the front and back, and her wavy brown hair fixed in a bun. She also had white gloves on both hands and carried a woven basket with a big smile on her face when she saw me. Little did I know that when she became that age, she looked just like I had pictured her in that dream.

Brandy was born on May 28, 1982. I believe I had the same nervousness as I did when my son was born, wondering how I was going to make it with two kids. But once again, this would fuel me to really get it together, despite some of the stupid mistakes I made in the past. I remember being in the delivery room as Deanne's labor pains became closer, as we prepared for Brandy's entrance into the world.

Unlike my son's birth, this time I was right there in the room watching every step of the arrival. When I should have been comforting my wife, I was the one who became overwhelmed and nearly fainted watching all this take place! But when Brandy finally came into the world, the joy of holding Brandy for the first time will be a moment I will never forget. Brandy was a beautiful baby girl! Very fair skin with adorable, fat cheeks and beautiful brown eyes. Having Brandy wasn't exactly planned, but an awesome surprise. Having a family became my why in life, which meant I had to take things more seriously at 21 and make it in the career I loved.

* * *

Taurus soon got very serious about making me the exclusive voice for their concert promotions. Competition in the concert business was becoming quite strong, and they needed to keep their brand identity intact. I went on to do concert spots for artists like Teddy Pendergrass and his infamous Ladies Night-Out Tour; I also voiced ads for Peabo Bryson, Gladys Knight, The Temptations, Smokey Robinson, Rick James, The Isley Brothers, and Earth, Wind & Fire, just to name a few.

Billy Sparks had a great relationship with WLBS and often visited the radio station. His loud voice and personality lit up the building, and when he visited, everyone knew Billy Sparks was around. He was an expert at getting all the radio people excited about the shows he was promoting, and he did it brilliantly! In 1982, Billy came to the station to introduce us to some new music from an artist simply known as Prince. Billy had already been on WGPR to get some airplay for the new artist on Mojo's show, but he needed more airplay. Our station was a little more conservative, though, so it was not easy getting Brent Wilson to sign off on such a controversial artist like Prince. However, after a few laughs and assurances, Billy convinced Brent and the management with his larger-than-life personality. We played a few songs off Prince's LP, focusing on two hit songs, "It's Gonna Be Lonely" and "I Wanna Be Your Lover."

Taurus Productions eventually brought Prince to Detroit for several concerts, and I was on hand to voice all the commercials. Billy and Quinten had a way of pushing the envelope when they promoted shows. To push a show, they even matched up Prince and Rick James on the same bill. They did whatever it took to get people's attention, buy the concert tickets, and fill the seats.

For this concert promo, they played up a battle of talent between Rick James and Prince, and all the radio commercials were designed to push that narrative. They called the concert "The Battle Royale at Cobo Hall!" I found myself wondering if the artists were even aware that the concert was being billed as a battle. The people were aware, though! Every place in Detroit was filled with talk of the battle between Rick James and Prince. We spent days in the booth creating the radio commercials for this show. The wording went something like this:

"Who will be the winner in the battle royale?"
"You be the judge!"
"Is it Prince or Rick James!"
"Get your tickets..."

Each ticket was $11.50, and the concert completely sold out. Rumor has it that Prince won.

Also in 1982, Earth, Wind, and Fire released "Let's Groove," and Billy and Quinten booked them for a show at Cobo Hall. The group was one of my all-time favorites, and I was excited to produce the radio spots for the show. As usual, Billy would sometimes show up at the station after my 2 am shift, and we would work on the commercials together.

The *Star Wars* movie was popular at the time, and we decided to describe a laser light show in one of the commercials. Earth, Wind, and Fire were known for opening with a magical display that left the audience in awe, and we used similar mystical laser sound effects in the production, with the line, *"See an amazing light show and be there as the musical gods disappear..."* The "disappear" at the end had multiple echoes before fading out at the end of the 60-second spot. Well, the only problem was that some folks were looking forward to seeing this "disappearing" act during the concert. But this never happened, leaving some people disappointed afterwards. Still, it was a hugely successful show with a vast number of ticket sales. Billy and Quinten were wizards of concert advertising, and their crazy ideas always worked brilliantly.

Prince went on to become a national sensation, and Taurus Productions became his exclusive promoters, taking him on concert tours across the country. I remained the go-to commercial spot producer for Billy. And they brought me on to voice and produce several national radio commercials for these tours. These commercials were quite special, and each one sounded spectacular thanks to Billy's ideas, my script, and my voice. As Prince's musical career continued to rise, several tours followed. First, it was the *Dirty Mind* tour, followed by the *Controversy* tour, the *1999* tour, and then *Purple Rain*. Prince topped all the charts across the nation.

I will never forget Billy Sparks showing up in an all-purple van with purple velvet seats which Prince purchased for Billy to promote his shows and music as he traveled across the country. To celebrate the massive success of the *Purple Rain* tour, Prince gave all his radio DJs and supporters an official *Purple Rain* tour jacket with our names embroidered in front. Billy Sparks also went on to appear in the 1984 movie, *Purple Rain*. This was an impressive feat for all of us in Detroit as we were proud to see one of our own starring in the number one box office movie. Billy played the owner of First Avenue Night Club, a shrewd, no-nonsense businessman who threatened Prince whenever he didn't perform up to par. Billy played the character perfectly, and all of us back in Detroit were impressed by his excellent acting skills

* * *

By 1984, the music scene shifted again, and WLBS began to record low ratings. Coupled with the rise of new radio stations like WJLB FM98 and 93FM WDRQ, WLBS 102.7's management decided to abandon the urban format that had worked for us in the past and switch to a punk rock format. For the first time since I was hired, I began to have some doubts about my career at WLBS.

A few days later, I was switched to the overnight 2 am to 6 am air shift. This was the graveyard shift, which meant I was not important enough to be heard as one of the DJs who would help the station attract a new audience. And maybe they were right, I knew nothing about the new wave punk rock music. On the new shift, I was made to play music of groups I had never heard before. Being made to play artists like Oingo Boingo, The Violent Femmes, The Clash, Stray Cats, Thomas Dolby, and New Order, I felt like a fish out of water.

Mike Halloran had the 10 pm to 2 am slot, right before mine. He was the most popular jock on the station, and he brought a large audience from his previous shift at another public radio station. His specialty was the new wave of music played in metro Detroit, and I did my best to learn from him. Mike stayed overnight on some nights just to help me know the main players in new wave music. The two of us became great friends as we worked back-to-back shifts.

One day, my son, Jaz, was singing "The Rubber Tree Plant" song around the house, and I had the great idea to record his voice. The song was taught to him by his mother, and I brought him to the station and recorded his version of the song. When Mike heard Jaz's adorable voice, he had the great idea to feature his recording after his show. Every single night, just before he went off the air, after playing all this new wave of punk music, Mike would sign off with the sweet innocent voice of Jaz singing:

"You got high hopes, you got high hopes.
"You got the high apple pie in the sky hopes.
"So any time you're getting' low,
"Instead of letting go,
"Just remember that ant.
"Ooops! There goes another rubber tree plant."

Things God Said to Me:

"*The biggest preparation is having faith in what I have called you to do.*
This is all trust. Learning who you should deal with and who not to.
Learning the discernment of character.
It's all part of the process before I can place you where you need to be.
"*Know that I'm with you always. You can talk to me anytime.*
Believe when I say in my word that I'm ordering your steps.
Doors are opening up supernaturally.
I am God. Remember what I have done.
I'm making a way for you.
Keep pushing, keep praying.
Stay in touch with me, as I will show you the way to go."

Chapter Eight

GOD HELP ME

Knowing that my days were limited at WLBS, I began looking at other stations where I believed I would be a better fit. While still making extra income producing radio commercials for concerts with Billy Sparks and Quinten Perry, I landed a part-time job at WDRQ 93FM in Southfield, a suburb just outside Detroit. Times were tight financially, but somehow, even though things were tough, we managed to make ends meet.

At WDRQ, I worked various fill-in shifts under our program director, Jim Snowden, also known as "The Snowman." Jim was a great inspiration to me. I marveled at his radio production skills, especially in crafting station imaging, the powerful station identification promos that made WDRQ stand out. I remember hearing promos like: "You're listening to WDRQ 93FM, number one for R&B!" The station was always giving away money and even cars, and Jim's production work made those moments electrifying.

A typical promo would go something like this:

"WDRQ is giving away thousands and thousands of dollars every day!" Then, a prerecorded phone call would play: "I won! Oh wow! I can't believe I won!" Jim's voice would then come back to wrap it up: "Your chance to win is coming up next on 93FM WDRQ."

I was fascinated by these promos. They opened my eyes to another area of radio production, incorporating listener voices into my work. Looking back, I believe these innovative promos from stations like WDRQ and WJLB in the '80s set a precedent for radio stations across the country.

I worked with a great team of radio personalities at WDRQ, including The Snowman, who did the morning show, as well as Mike Straford, Chris McClendon, Jay Michael McKay, Aubrey Lee, and Rick Roberts. Rick, who was from St. Louis, only worked at the station briefly, but I'll never forget him telling me he knew the legendary Funkateer George Clinton, who lived in Detroit at the time. One day, Rick invited me to join him at a studio where George was working on a song. George was a friendly, down-to-earth guy, not as wild as you'd expect despite his colorful hair and outrageous music. After the session, the three of us piled into my car, a little blue 1975 Beetle. That night happened to be one of the coldest ever, with temperatures well below zero. Unfortunately, my car had no heat! I remember George and Rick shivering and complaining all the way to their destinations.

WDRQ 93.1 jumped into an urban/Black Contemporary format in 1982 and caught fire in 1982-83, which set up a head-to-head with WJLB FM 98. Newspapers in '83 framed it as a real battle, and WJLB countered hard by retooling the sound and luring key talent (e.g., the Electrifying Mojo) to strengthen nights and weekend mix shows.

By spring 1985, the fight was effectively over: WDRQ abandoned urban and flipped to soft AC as WLTI (Lite FM) in April 1985. Once WDRQ exited, WJLB consolidated the urban audience and went on to dominate the lane through the late '80s, labeling themselves as "Detroit's Strongest Songs!"

After the plummet of WDRQ and its urban format, I was forced to find work elsewhere. I eventually took a job at WDKX in Rochester,

New York. This new environment came with fresh experiences and opportunities, and I was determined to make my mark as always. Rochester, a mid-sized market in upstate New York, had a significant Hispanic and African American population, many of whom had migrated from New York City.

WDKX was one of the first Black-owned radio stations in the country, founded by Andrew Langston. Keeping with its urban contemporary format, WDKX's call letters were chosen to honor Black heroes: W for radio stations east of the Mississippi, D for Frederick Douglass, K for Martin Luther King Jr., and X for Malcolm X. In our staff meetings, Mr. Langston always reminded us of this history and the sacrifices he made to establish and sustain the station.

The program director, his son Andre Langston Jr., also known as Andre Marcel, assigned me the 7 pm to midnight shift. My on-air name was Commander McBride, Commander of the Airwaves. We lived in a very nice two-bedroom condo on the outskirts of Rochester. The price was a little high, but we tried our best to make it work. Deanne babysat for a couple of neighborhood kids while I got a little extra work in some local nightclubs spinning records. I also got a part-time job at the mall working for a clothing store called Merry-Go-Round. I was a salesman working under a bunch of teenage girls who were the supervisors. Here I was, 22 years old, being bossed around by some teenagers. This was pretty degrading! Needless to say, this job didn't last long for me. But I had to do what I had to do to survive.

One night after I came home from my late shift at the station, I immediately got into bed. I may have been asleep for about an hour when Deanne woke me up. "Gerald, wake up! I think I hear something."

Half asleep, I said, "What is it?"

She said, "I don't know. You need to get up and see what it is. It sounds like it's coming from the basement."

I got up to make my way down to the basement. Unfortunately, the only light was a chain light that was right in the middle of the basement.

It was pitch black as I tried to find my way to the light. The basement floor was covered with the kids' toys. As I stepped around and dodged the sharp toy objects that stabbed my bare feet, I was still reaching in the dark, trying to find the string attached to the light so I could see. All of a sudden, before I could find the light, I ran right into the support beam pole of the basement. Bam! I hit the pole so hard it almost knocked me out! Still staggering, I finally found the string to the light. There was no sign of anything in the basement that might be the noise my wife had heard. But I did discover that my t-shirt and face were full of blood from running into the basement support pole.

When I returned, staggering up the stairs back into the bedroom, all bloody, Deanne went into a panic! "Oh my God! Call the police! Call the police!"

I responded, "Don't call the police."

"What happened?" she asked. "I ran into the pole in the basement." Relieved it wasn't a burglary, she then burst out into laughter. I also could only laugh at myself.

By 1985, rap music was well established, even though I initially thought it was just a passing fad. I remember playing Sugar Hill Gang's "Rapper's Delight," which borrowed from Chic's "Good Times," and thinking this genre wouldn't last. I was proven wrong as our Rochester listeners couldn't get enough of the new hip-hop sound. Our playlist included artists like Run-DMC, Doug E. Fresh, The Real Roxanne, LL Cool J, UTFO, Steady B, and The Fat Boys, to name a few. These artists frequently made tour stops in Rochester, and during the summer, the *Fresh Fest* tour rolled into town with LL Cool J, Beastie Boys, Run-DMC, Doug E. Fresh, and The Fat Boys. To promote the show, the station organized an outdoor event featuring an eating contest between The Fat Boys and WDKX's radio personalities. Needless to say, The Fat Boys won, devouring more hamburgers than we could even attempt.

Despite my passion for radio, money was still tight. My salary at WDKX was about $600 every two weeks. Mr. Langston always wanted to make sure we appreciated the pay. Every payday, he would call a staff meeting to discuss the struggles he faced to become one of the first black radio station owners. However, while I appreciated the history and the privilege of being part of such a legendary station, it didn't help when my bills exceeded my paycheck. My $500-a-month condo rent, car note, and expenses for my family of four made it difficult to stay afloat. At one point, I fell behind on rent for two months. Notices from the leasing company came and went, but I was completely unprepared when a bailiff showed up at my door.

"Are you Gerald McBride?" he asked.

"Yes," I replied.

"We have a notice to evict you today."

I feigned surprise. "Really?" as if I hadn't seen it coming. My mind raced at the thought of being put out on the street with all our belongings. It was unthinkable. I had to act fast. "Is there any way you could give me a little more time?" I asked.

The bailiff looked past me into the living room, where my children were playing. He paused, then said, "I'll give you until 5 pm today," before walking away.

I remember driving to the station and saying the only prayer I knew at the time: "God, please help me." That was the best I could do. "God, please help me," I kept whispering.

Asking Mr. Langston for money wasn't an easy thing, especially after hearing about how he had built WDKX against all odds, overcoming racism and financial barriers, and he never missed an opportunity to remind us of the hardships he endured. When I entered his office, he was focused on some paperwork, barely looking up.

"Mr. Langston?" I knocked lightly on the door, which was already half-open.

He glanced at me but said nothing. His face was buried behind a pile of papers.

"Could I talk to you for a moment?" I asked.

"Come in," he responded.

I stood there, unsure if he even knew who I was. Our paths rarely crossed, as I usually dealt with his son, the program director. This was the first time I would talk to him face-to-face.

Finally, I gathered my courage and spoke. "Mr. Langston, a bailiff came to my house this morning. They're going to put me and my family out on the street. I'm two months behind on rent. Is there any way I could get an advance on my pay?"

Silence filled the room.

Then, as expected, he launched into a speech about his struggles: "As the President of NABOB, I fought to get this radio station. There were no Black-owned radio stations when I started. I worked hard to get this one in Rochester."

I listened respectfully, though I wasn't sure how this related to my eviction. When he finally finished, he said, "See Mrs. Langston. She will issue you a check."

I had heard his speech many times before, but this time, it resonated differently. His hard work and sacrifice had paved the way for many Black-owned radio stations and provided employment for people like me.

In that moment, I was also grateful for one more thing: God had heard the only prayer I knew at the time, "Please, help me."

Things God spoke to me:

"The Holy Spirit is always with you.
Learn to listen to the still soft voice that speaks loud and clear.
You know it. You just have to focus on it.
I am so pleased with you, for the time you spend with me.
This is the most important thing.
Because of this, everything else falls into place.
Remember my scripture.
Seek first my kingdom and all these things shall be added.
I can trust you, Gerald. Watch what I will do.
You know my voice. Trust me, Gerald. You know my voice.
I will continue to speak to you. Walk with me, Gerald, in this place.
Get me involved in all you do. I love this language you speak.
Know that a great harvest is coming.
You are my obedient son. You know my voice.
Teach others to know my voice."

Chapter Nine

TV Shows

My stay at WDKX in Rochester lasted about a year before I moved back to Flint. I returned to WDZZ to do mid-days under the programming of the Flint legend, Sam Williams. At that time, the station introduced an automation tape system, meaning all the music was pre-selected, eliminating the use of turntables and records. This was a major adjustment for me. While I had previously worked with formatted playlists, I still had some flexibility to insert my creativity by adding or substituting songs when I felt it was appropriate. I had always believed I had a good sense of what listeners wanted and how the music should flow.

However, this automation system was different. There was absolutely no way for callers to make requests and expect to hear their songs played. The music selection felt off, and I had no opportunity to influence what was played. These became some of the most frustrating days of my career. I felt stifled, and for the first time, I lacked enthusiasm for my work. My side hustle of recording commercials dwindled to almost nothing as companies like Taurus Productions and others sought services elsewhere.

Moving between Rochester and Flint cost me valuable contacts for extra work. Looking back, I now understand that before making any career moves, it is crucial to seek guidance from the Lord. Yet, even if you make a misstep, God has a way of redirecting you to the right path, because He loves you that much.

Later in 1986, I received a call from Joe Spencer, program director of WGPR radio and Channel 62 TV in Detroit. He offered me a job as head of radio production and an assistant in programming. I jumped at the opportunity, which came with a $20,000-a-year salary, and my family and I moved back to Detroit. My job involved recording voiceovers, adding music to commercials, and ensuring they aired according to the program log. Most of these commercials were pre-recorded national spots for major companies like Burger King, McDonald's, Art Van Furniture, and various gas and electric companies. WGPR had a legendary lineup of radio personalities, including JC Cage in the morning, Marvelous Marv in the midday, Clarence "Foody" Rome in the afternoon, Henry Tyler from 7 pm to midnight, and Reggie Brown on overnights.

Unlike the rigid automation system at WDZZ, WGPR's DJs had the freedom to play whatever they wanted, creating a unique sound that truly represented Detroit's rich musical heritage. With my production and voiceover skills, Joe asked me to help shape the station's sound through imaging, creating station IDs and promos to run between songs and commercial breaks. One example was, "You're listening to Detroit's number one radio station, WGPR 107.5." Several variants of these imaging elements helped define the station's identity and maintain consistency. I also incorporated listener testimonials, a technique I had learned while working at WDRQ, which helped drive high ratings.

Joe was pleased with the fresh sound I brought to WGPR and soon added me to the station's on-air lineup as the morning show host. The other DJs were moved to different time slots, marking the first time WGPR had a full-fledged morning show. I built a team that included Fonda Thomas for traffic, Harold Sullivan for news, and my sidekick, Joe Goldbock. Our morning show quickly became a success, waking the city of Detroit with news, traffic, information, and comedic segments. One of my most popular creations was a character played by Joe Goldbock called "The Boss." Every morning, listeners would hear the blaring ring of the hotline, signaling that The Boss was about to call in with ridiculous demands. The segment was hilarious and quickly became a listener favorite.

In 1986, when the Pope visited the United States, Detroit was one of the cities he visited. The morning show team decided to create something around this visit. We crafted a skit where The Boss demanded that I get the Pope on my show. It was all in good fun, but the general manager misunderstood the bit, thinking we were mocking him by making these demands. As a result, management abruptly canceled the morning show and removed us from the air. WGPR management wasn't familiar with this kind of radio and didn't understand that skits ran on morning radio shows like this as part of the entertainment.

Joe Spencer was deeply disappointed by this decision and fought for me, explaining that the character was purely fictional and not intended as a jab at management. However, the decision stood. What did emerge from these discussions, though, was a new opportunity for me.

WGPR wasn't just a radio station; it was also home to America's first African American-owned TV station, Channel 62. For years, the station had aired *The Scene*, a popular local dance show hosted by Nat Morris. Major African American celebrities visiting Detroit always made a stop at WGPR for interviews. Legends like Stevie Wonder, Smokey Robinson, LL Cool J, Will Smith, Gladys Knight, Pam Grier, The Jacksons, The Time, Earth, Wind & Fire, and Luther Vandross all passed through.

However, after I was taken off the air, a dispute between Nat Morris and WGPR management led to *The Scene's* cancellation, leaving a void in the 6 pm time slot. Joe Spencer called me into his office and said, "I think I have the perfect opportunity for you. How would you like to host and produce a TV show to replace *The Scene*?" I had no experience in television, but I didn't have much choice. It was either take this role or lose my job. So, of course, I said yes!

Joe guided me through every step of creating a television show, from concept development to set design, assembling a production crew, creating a format, auditioning dancers, setting up lighting, and everything else a TV show required. It was a crash course in TV production. We wanted to make this new dance show distinct from its predecessor, so we revamped the set and rebranded the program as *Contempo*. The show featured the *Contempo* dancers, the latest music videos, and performances from both local and national artists, with me as the host.

Hosting *Contempo* allowed me to introduce a young, up-and-coming comedian named Tim Allen. As we all know now, Tim would later become a major Hollywood star as *The Tim Allen Show* took off, starring Tim as the Tool Man. Another guest was a fresh-faced 18-year-old rapper promoting his first hit, "Parents Just Don't Understand." He had an infectious energy and a funny personality. Backing him up on the turntables was his DJ, Jazzy Jeff. Of course, this duo was none other than The Fresh Prince, Will Smith, and DJ Jazzy Jeff. Smith would go on to become one of Hollywood's biggest stars.

This unexpected dive into television turned out to be a valuable learning experience, one I now realize was orchestrated by God for a greater purpose in my future. One day at the station, I ran into Quinten Perry, whom I hadn't seen in years. During our conversation, he said something that changed my life forever.

"I just left Houston, Texas, where I visited Bill Young Productions for my radio and TV spots. They have an incredible production studio, and they handle commercials for everyone," he told me. Then he added, "This is what you should be doing."

The moment he said that, something clicked. It was an "aha" moment when everything became clear and certain, and I faced an undeniable truth about the path I needed to take. In retrospect, I now see that God was speaking through Quinten about my future. It was a confirmation that a talent I had within me had become dormant, but that would soon change.

After about a year, financial issues forced *Contempo* off the air, and my position at the station was reduced to part-time, with a salary barely above minimum wage. Supporting a family of four on that income was impossible, so I had to find another job. I landed a part-time weekend overnight shift at WHYT 96.3 FM. It was a pop station, but about 85% of its music was R&B. Despite having an all-white on-air staff, the station still maintained a pop sound that appealed to its audience. My shift ran from 2 am to 6 am on Saturdays and Sundays, which was the dreaded graveyard shift. At just $10 an hour, this job wasn't enough to sustain my family. I needed another source of income. And those words from Quinten Perry kept echoing in my mind. Thus, I knew I needed to start my own production studio.

Things God spoke to me:

*"Know how much I love you, Gerald.
Nothing can separate me from you.
What happens when you drink alcohol?
You grieve the Holy Spirit from speaking through you,
and hearing him speak to you.
Alcohol is known as a spirit.
Just like the spirit of God can guide your thoughts
and the words that come out of your mouth,
so can alcohol in the opposite way."*

Chapter Ten

✝

My Big Bold Steps

In 1987, almost out of desperation, I started Sounds Good Studio from the attic of my small bungalow on the east side of Detroit. I borrowed $1,500 from my brother Marvin, and a friend, Jay Dixon, a very talented radio production manager for WJLB, gave me a few pieces of equipment. With two reel-to-reel tape recorders, a mixing board, speakers, an SXP 90 effects unit, and a mic, I was ready to go. Only one problem stood between me and this great adventure: I couldn't get all this equipment to work right. Every time I recorded something, it came out muffled.

I finally landed my first paying client. My assignment was to create an ad for a fashion show at Ford Auditorium. I worked on the radio spot over and over until it finally sounded halfway decent, and it made it to the airwaves. My first pay was $75 for Sounds Good Studio.

Running my own business taught me that, sometimes in life, when our backs are against the wall, desperation pushes us into our destiny. My lesson was to keep working at it until I got it right, especially when I knew it was part of my purpose. You must be persistent and determined. Keep at it, and eventually, it will all come together for the good. I began landing a few freelance jobs here and there, but between my part-time job at WHYT and the little I was making with Sounds Good Studio, things were still tight for us. After a few months, I finally figured out how to create a decent sound with the equipment I had, and business started to pick up.

A playwright named Mike Matthews reached out to me about creating some commercials for a project he was working on. I will always remember that first meeting we had in my attic studio. Mike had created a stage play called *Mama Don't*, which was embarking on a 50-city tour, and he wanted to hire me to produce the radio spots for each market. He showed up with a cassette tape of one-line soundbites from the script and wanted me to incorporate them into a radio commercial.

This was my first introduction to producing radio spots for the Black theater circuit, better known as the Chitlin' Circuit. In 60 seconds, my job was to pull the audience into the plot of the play using these various sound bites from the actors, with background music to enhance the drama. Think about a movie trailer, but in this case, it was for stage plays. At fifty dollars a spot for 50 cities, this turned out to be a great business deal, and it became my first national tour, producing radio spots, which served as the perfect springboard for establishing Sounds Good Studio.

It was also the beginning of something bigger than I could have imagined. The Black theater market took off, becoming a major source of entertainment for African American audiences.

In 1988, I received a call from James Alexander asking if I would be interested in an assistant radio production job at WJLB. I was raising a family and needed all the financial resources I could get. So, of course, I took the job. They offered $26,000-a-year, but beyond this good pay, this was my dream station. It was the WJLB radio station that I grew up listening to; it was the place that had inspired me to pursue radio. I had even started there as a Soul Teen Reporter under Donnie Simpson. Now, my dream was becoming a reality. Needless to say, I was determined to maximize the opportunity with excellence.

Production at WJLB was very demanding. As a top-rated radio station, the volume of commercials that had to be created and dubbed for air was overwhelming for just two people: Dave Mitchell and me. One day, James assigned me to the weekend shift, and I was thrilled to do more prominent work.

One Saturday afternoon during my shift, a promoter named Al Haymon visited me at the station. Al had a young group from his hometown of Boston that he wanted to introduce to the station. Their music had a bubblegum pop feel, similar to the Jackson 5 when they first started. Their debut song was "Candy Girl," and the group was called New Edition. I would have never thought this young group of guys would be the superstar group that they became. It goes to show you that you can never underestimate small beginnings, which would be something I would learn about myself as well.

I had worked part-time for a few months before the station offered me the midday shift, paying $35,000-a-year. Our air staff at WJLB was considered an all-star lineup with Mason & Company from 6 am to 10 am, me from 10 am to 3 pm, Chris McClendon from 3 pm to 7 pm, Special K from 7 pm to midnight, and Johnny "Smooth" Edwards on overnights. This ensemble also had the top ratings in the market to prove it. One thing we could always count on back then was getting all the stars. A variety of musicians and celebrities graced our studios at WJLB with their presence for interviews, and our station was considered an efficient way to generate sales for their latest single or LP.

I remember doing many interviews with various artists while at WJLB. One that stands out was with Natalie Cole. She was in Detroit promoting her latest single, "I Live for Your Love." I had prepared for the interview days ahead of time and was nervous about speaking with the legendary Natalie Cole. However, when she arrived at the studio, she seemed unhappy about being there. Her answers were brief and vague. Years later, I would understand why. Natalie was struggling with a terrible drug addiction that nearly ruined her career.

One of my best interviews, however, was with Roger Troutman of the group Zapp. I believe Roger was one of the first to introduce the talk box to R&B radio with hits like "More Bounce to the Ounce," "I Heard It Through the Grapevine," and "A Touch of Jazz." When he arrived at the studio, he brought a keyboard and his infamous talk box. Whenever I or a caller asked him a question, he would respond through the talk box. He was an incredibly talented artist. It was a tragedy to learn years later that his own brother murdered him in a family dispute.

Talking to listeners on the request line was always interesting. Back then, it was the easiest way for the audience to reach their favorite radio personalities. The phone lines were always lit up with callers requesting songs, trying to win money or concert tickets, or simply saying how much they enjoyed the show. One particular call stood out in my time at WJLB. One day, while I was on the air, a man called from Chandler Park.

I answered the request line: "WJLB, hello caller."

The man responded, "Hey, I'm in my car in Chandler Park, and I'm about to shoot myself."

I was too stunned to speak. There was a long pause. I was caught completely off guard. Finally, I said, "Wait! Did you just say you were about to kill yourself?"

"Yes," he replied, his voice was firm, but pained.

In all my years on the radio and the countless people I had spoken to on the request line, I had never encountered anything like this. I knew I had to act fast.

"Wait a minute," I said. "Let me get you some help. Nothing is worth killing yourself over."

"I can't take it anymore," he answered me.
"Where exactly are you?" I asked.
"In Chandler Park."
"Where in Chandler Park?" I pressed.
"Near the golf course."

As he explained his location, I discreetly recorded our conversation while continuing to talk to him. I put him on hold, called 911, and directed emergency responders to where he was in the park. When I returned to the line, he was still there, but then he said he had to go and abruptly hung up. To this day, I have no idea whether the police made it in time or if anything I said convinced him to change his mind.

In 1989, I received an offer to join WJZZ radio in Detroit, owned by Bell Broadcasting, one of the few African American-owned stations at the time. WJZZ was a station I had always admired and grew up listening to, featuring a mix of fusion jazz artists like George Duke, Herbie Hancock, Stanley Clarke, Donald Byrd, Phyllis Hyman, and Norman Connors. It wasn't the old-school classic jazz but a more contemporary, hip sound that resonated with the times. The job seemed like the perfect fit. They offered me $60,000 to do the morning show, which was a huge jump from the $35,000 I was making at WJLB. Without a contract, I accepted the position, which, in hindsight, was unprofessional.

The WJZZ morning show consisted of me, Lloyd Jackson handling news, and Mark Unger covering sports. Unlike WJLB, which had a strict playlist and format, WJZZ gave its on-air personalities more freedom in music selection. As long as the songs were available in the studio, we could create our own flow. For example, if I played three jazz instrumentals, I could use my creativity to mix in a vocal track here and there to keep the rhythm engaging. They encouraged us to craft a smooth and seamless listening experience. At WJZZ, I had the privilege of working alongside some legendary jazz radio personalities, including Rosetta Hines, Cliff Coleman, and Larry "Doc" Elliott.

However, my time at WJZZ was short. In 1990, WMXD Mix 92.3, owned by Fritz Broadcasting in Southfield, offered me a morning show position with an $80,000 salary plus bonuses, an offer I couldn't refuse. It was the most I had ever been paid in radio. And with Sounds Good Studio also taking off, things were looking better than ever. My new shift at WMXD was from 6 am to 10 am, and I co-hosted with Kathy Young Welch, a well-known and highly respected newscaster in Detroit.

Things God spoke to me:

*"You know my voice. You know I am guiding you.
Gerald, know that I'm with you in every part of your life.
I am a rewarder of those who diligently seek me.
You are seeing the results of that.
Keep seeking me. I have so much more for you.
You are living out my word. It is important to read
my word,
but what's more important is to live it out in your life
each and every day.
Don't just read it, live it."*

Chapter Eleven

Struggles and Turning Points

Things seemed to be going great in my radio career. After years of barely making ends meet and making so many sacrifices, everything was finally paying off. As business grew, I was able to move Sounds Good Studio out of the attic and into a small space in Southfield, sharing it with another studio owned by Lee Norris.

Though my career was taking off, my personal life was falling apart. Deanne and I divorced, and it became a pivotal moment in my life. Separated from my family, I began seeking God like never before, desperate for answers. This was one of the most painful moments of my life, and the only thing that seemed to offer any hope was finding a real connection with God.

The only church I knew at the time was the Catholic church, where my mother used to take us as kids. I went back to Madonna Church, hoping God would meet me there, searching for direction, or for anything that would make sense of what I was going through. I would show up early on weekday mornings and find nuns praying the rosary. I hadn't prayed the rosary in years, but somehow, I remembered the words:

> *Hail Mary, full of grace, the Lord is with thee. Blessed art thou amongst women and blessed is the fruit of thy womb, Jesus. Holy Mary, Mother of God, pray for us sinners, now and at the hour of our death. Amen.*

At the time, this was all I knew to do. I didn't know if my prayers were making a difference, but it was the beginning of my search, the start of a deep hunger to know God.

More than anything, I missed the time I spent with Jaz and Brandy every day. Now, all I had were the weekends, and those days became my most anticipated moments. I was filled with great joy and hope again as I spent time with them. I didn't know if they understood the pain I was carrying, but their presence always brought some relief. Dropping them off at their mother's house, though, was unbearable.

One day, after leaving them, I pulled over to the side of the road, overcome with emotion. The weight of being separated from my family was too much. My thoughts became dark, and for the first time, I questioned whether my life was worth living.

"God, where are you?" I cried out. "Please help me! This hurts, Lord, and I don't know what to do."

I sat there, crying, feeling completely lost. It was the lowest moment of my life.

I was a morning show host with the most important shift on WMXD at the time. Each morning, I had to go on the radio and pretend everything was fine. My job was to cheerfully wake up the city and encourage everyone to have a great day. "Good morning, rise and shine! This is going to be the best day of your life! Here's Peabo Bryson's "Can You Stop the Rain?"" As Peabo sang this song of sorrow, it only reminded me of my troubles. So, in between songs, I could barely hold myself together. I would put my head down on the console, fighting back the weight of my emotions.

Off the air, my co-host and others in the studio had begun to sense something was wrong, but I never let on how deep the pain really was. At that moment, I knew my life had to change. I talked to many friends, hoping for guidance, but in the end, I knew that only God had the answer. I couldn't do this without God. He was the only one who had the answers, the guidance on what to do, and how to handle this crisis in my life. He had to be at the center of my decisions from this point forward. I'm convinced now that God meets us right where we are.

Sometimes, it is the deep, painful disappointments that bring us closest to Him because that's when He has our full attention. We have all had our wake-up calls, and it is in those moments that we truly learn who God is, His love, and what it means to trust Him completely. It is a lifelong process, one that I am still walking through to this day. A friend of mine once asked me about his son, wondering when he might start taking life more seriously. I told him that for me, things didn't start changing until I was in my early 30s.

As I talked to more people, I realized it was a common turning point. In our 20s, we're still trying to figure life out—careers, direction, identity. But in our 30s, reality starts to set in. We start to feel like we don't have time to waste.

* * *

Now in my early 30s, I found myself moving back home with my parents. It felt a bit degrading to have to go back home from where I started. Even though my mother and father accepted me with welcoming arms, it felt strange to be a grown man going back to page one. Here I am sleeping in my twin-size bunk bed, looking up at the slats of the upper bunk. But because of my finances and my obligation to ensure my kids maintained their lifestyle in the house I had provided for them and their mother, and could continue attending St. Matthews, the private Catholic school they attended, I had to make the sacrifice.

My parents had been discussing the idea of downsizing and moving to a small apartment for the two of them. And after I had been at my mother's house for a couple of months, instead of putting the house on the market, it was offered to each sibling who might be interested. I wasn't in a financial position to buy the house. The only sibling that it made sense for was my younger sister Julie, who jumped at the chance to buy this home in the university district of Detroit, where we all grew up. So after a couple of months, the deal went through, and the house was sold to her. But what about me? Well, I'm glad you asked. Julie allowed me to stay for two months until I could save enough to get my own place. I loved my sister, but living with her was another thing! So even two months was too long!

In just a few weeks, I moved into a two-bedroom apartment in downtown Detroit at River Place Apartments. One room was my bedroom, and the other was my recording studio. This became my new home, my new workspace, and every weekend, Jaz and Brandy would come stay with me. They loved coming downtown, not just to be with me but because there was always a gang of kids running in and out of the apartment, giving the place a community feel. During the week, though, it was just me and God.

That time alone became invaluable. I woke up every morning with nothing but silence and the presence of God. It was during this time that I got baptized, fully committing my life to Christ. Instead of a church, my baptism took place in the community pool at River Place Apartments, led by a friend who had helped guide me to the Lord. Soon after, I found myself visiting different churches, hoping to find a church home. This isn't a put-down to Catholic churches, but I felt like I needed more this time. I wanted to dig deeper into scriptures and get a better understanding of who God is and what he expects of me. I had a burning desire to learn more about my spiritual walk. I spent several months going from church to church. Some were too loud, some seemed chaotic, with people who were "hooping and hollering" and running up and down the aisle. For me, as a new Christian, it seemed a little overwhelming! I know people were filled with the Holy Ghost, but for a new believer, I was wondering what in the heck was going on in there!

A friend of mine, Sterlene Cannon, called and invited me to attend her church, Word of Faith International Christian Center, on the corner of Nevada and Vandyke Street in Detroit. I'll never forget my first time walking into Word of Faith on a Sunday morning. This church seemed very different. It had some of the same Holy Ghost excitement, but very organized. It was packed. I could barely find a seat, but an usher went out of his way to help me find a place. He seated me in the back on the main floor, under the balcony that hung over half of the main floor.

As the congregation was fired up in praise and worship, with everyone standing and praising God in this electric atmosphere, I could see the balcony bouncing up and down right above our heads. I could see the balcony actually moving! Yes, moving! Think about it, while I'm trying to get into the service, I couldn't help but notice this balcony rocking. I'm thinking, is this safe? There are people up there! What if this balcony came crashing down on top of all of us! Honestly, this was a little nerve-wracking for a first-time visitor. What I would eventually learn was that the engineers had designed the balcony that way many years ago. And the bouncing is, in fact, what keeps it safe.

As I began listening to the message by Bishop Keith Butler, it seemed to be tailor-made for me, almost like he took a page out of my life.

Navigating this new chapter of my life, I found that every message from Bishop Keith Butler seemed to be exactly what I needed at that moment. It was as if God was speaking directly to me through every sermon, showing me how to find answers in His Word when I needed direction the most. That's when I knew I had found my church home. When every message feels like it was designed just for you, you know you're in the right place.

Things God spoke to me:

*"Know that I'm here and I'm so proud of you.
Remember these things you are doing for me and
the kingdom.
I will always take care of you. I know your needs
and desires.
You are my faithful son.
I am so pleased with everything you are doing as you are
guided by me.
I need more people to walk in my ways.
For I have a long life of prosperity for them.
Let your light shine, Gerald. Let it shine bright.
I'm guiding and directing you as you speak with others.
Trust me, Gerald."*

Chapter Twelve

✝

Legacy Born in a Small Apartment

This new season of my life felt like acceleration. As I surrendered control of my life and career to God, things seemed to take off for the business in ways I never imagined. I met Jeff Sharpe from Stage Right Productions, and through their contracts as promoters, I had the opportunity to do tour radio spots for some of the biggest names in music including: Luther Vandross, Barry White, Earth, Wind & Fire, The Isley Brothers, Anita Baker, Mary J. Blige, Destiny's Child (with Beyoncé), Gladys Knight, and more. Each time these opportunities came, I had to audition for the contract.

Effectively, at this time, there were only three major companies specializing in concert tour spots — Bill Young Productions, Tour

Design, and my company, now renamed Voice Over Productions. So, it all basically came down to who could produce the best commercial, which had to be approved by the artist's management. Because I had a deep, rich Black voice, while the other two companies primarily used a white male voice, I won most of the contracts for R&B shows.

My little apartment became a hub of constant activity during the week, with the studio running at full speed. When the kids came for their weekend visits, they found themselves right in the middle of it all. Brandy, at ten years old, loved spending time in the studio, learning the soundboard, recording her voice, and making tapes. It became her playground. She was always full of questions about the business, eager to understand how the equipment worked and how to create voiceovers. I even started using her for kids' commercials, and she quickly became skilled at it. Jaz, on the other hand, wasn't particularly interested in the technical or voiceover side, but he was drawn to the promotional aspect. Since most of my clients were promoters, he naturally picked up a lot from our conversations about marketing and advertising.

Looking back, I can clearly see God's hand in it all. Today, Brandy is thriving in the voiceover business and partners with me through her own company, Brandy Mitchell Design, producing video commercials for concert tours, with her work and voice recognized nationwide. Meanwhile, Jaz has built his own successful advertising agency, Adwater Media, with a roster of major clients.

Being a single parent during this period was critical to the development of my children. It forged a strong bond between us in that small apartment at River Place. By 1992, Voice Over Productions was flourishing. We became one of the top three radio and TV production houses in the nation for concert spots. While the other two companies were one-stop shops handling radio, TV, and graphic design, the majority of contracts for African American events were awarded to us. Our team was small but efficient. Greg Shelton handled traffic and deliveries, making daily trips to FedEx with reel-to-reel tapes for clients nationwide. Leon Reynolds assisted in production, bringing his creative touch to countless spots. Shannon Scott managed the office, accounting, and billing. Despite our size, we executed large contracts with quick turnarounds and consistently high-quality work.

In 1993, after a night with the kids at the movies, I had a dream. I saw myself meeting and dating a woman who lived on the east side of Detroit with her young daughter. I dream a lot, which sometimes means I might have had a little too much pizza before bed. But this particular dream seemed to be vividly real. Later in life, I would learn that these kinds of dreams should be written down. I read somewhere that it's important to keep a pen and pad on your nightstand, and when you wake up, write down the dream before you forget it, then examine it and pray about it to see if it was from God. This dream had that kind of significance.

I wasn't particularly interested in dating at the time. My life was very busy with VOP, doing my daily radio show, and keeping up with my kids, which kept me occupied. My assistant Greg Shelton saw me working all the time and said to me one day, "Man, you work too much. That's all you do is work."

I replied, "But I'm happy doing this."

"You need to go out on some dates."

It seemed like Greg wouldn't leave me alone about my single life.

One day, he said, "I have the perfect lady for you. Her name is Karen Wright."

I wasn't sure who she was because I had only met her once or twice. I immediately tried to picture her in my head. This would be like a blind date, which was all new to me after 14 years of marriage. Honestly, I just wasn't motivated, but because Greg was so persistent, I finally gave in as he arranged the date. I called Karen. Our conversation was very short, but Karen asked if we could meet for coffee. I agreed, and she suggested the Elmwood Grill. I hung up the phone and thought, "Coffee? I don't even drink coffee!"

A couple of days later, I met Karen at the Elmwood Grill right around the block from her job at the Music Hall. Karen sat there with her girlfriend as I walked up to the table. I startled her because I walked up on them suddenly, as they weren't paying attention.

"Excuse me. Are you Karen Wright?"

Looking surprised, she answered, "Yes. You must be Gerald." For some reason, this moment felt a little awkward. Karen excused herself from her friend, and we began our first date. Once I saw her, it all came back to me where I had seen her before. I remember seeing her once at one of my clients' offices as she walked out with her daughter, Alana, who must have been about five years old at the time, and I thought to myself, "What a beautiful lady with a cute little girl."

When I saw her at my client's office, we hadn't been introduced. It was just a polite hello. But needless to say, she was just as beautiful on the day we really met. Our first date was really just walking around downtown and talking, and then eventually making our way to my apartment, where it was business as usual with my small setup, preparing the packages of radio spots that needed to be shipped out that day. Karen and I really hit it off and decided we would like to continue getting to know each other a couple of days later with a date to the Detroit Grand Prix.

Karen often spoke about her daughter, whom I hadn't met yet because she was spending the summer with her grandparents in Beckley, West Virginia. A few weeks into dating, Karen asked if I would ride with her to pick up Alana. I thought it would be a great idea to turn it into a road trip for the kids, so I rented an RV, packed up Jaz and Brandy, and we headed south.

Weaving through the mountains and winding highways, the drive through the scenery was breathtaking. When we finally arrived in Beckley, we didn't stay long. As Karen gathered Alana's things, I waited in the RV with the kids. Then I saw her for the first time. She was a beautiful little brown-skinned girl with a poised and articulate voice. She was excited, partly because she was in an RV and partly because there were other kids on board. As we got back on the highway, we kept passing Cracker Barrel restaurants. Alana wanted to stop at one, but Karen refused. Jaz, being a 13-year-old boy, saw this as an opportunity to tease her. Every time we passed another Cracker Barrel, he would snicker and say, "There goes another Cracker Barrel!" This became their first inside joke and the start of their sibling bond.

Karen was a hardworking single mom. Newly divorced, she found herself—like so many others—working tirelessly to support her family. I watched her put in long hours, starting early each morning and often staying late into the night as the program director of a popular Detroit theatre, managing the shows she had booked. I always admired her work ethic, professionalism, and organizational skills as she also juggled the responsibility of taking care of Alana. After finishing her day at the Music Hall, she started helping me at Voice Over Productions in the evenings. I worked late nights as well, making sure commercials were done and ready for overnight delivery. Seeing Karen step in and support me like that showed me something different about the woman I was dating.

Karen jumped right in and helped me get organized. Not that I was doing a bad job, but with her expertise and attention to detail, she gave the business an updated shipping and receiving system and an invoicing system that took us to another level, which was much needed as my business was rapidly growing. She stepped in at the right time, setting this foundation for the business that would be helpful for years to come. Early on, Karen showed some of the qualities of a great helpmeet —a true Proverbs 31 woman. But for the moment, I wasn't quite ready to take the next big step; dating was just fine for me for now.

Meanwhile, the kids seemed to get along very well. We spent many weekends together. Every summer, one of our favorite things to do was spend the weekends at a friend's lake cottage we rented. The kids loved going there. We took not only them, but also some of their friends. It was a beautiful place with the cabins on a private lake where the kids would spend hours swimming, fishing, and enjoying campfires at night. I believe this gave all our kids an appreciation for God's gift of nature — the fresh air, the beautiful forest of trees outlining the private lake, and the beautiful drive through the country to get there. These would be some of our fondest memories of the summers we spent there.

In this same period, the Black theater industry was booming and had become one of the leading sources of entertainment for African Americans. Fortunately for me, my company became the voice behind many of these productions. In 1992, I met a young playwright and director named David E. Talbert. His first play, *Lord Have Mercy*, starred Morris Day of The Time. David approached me to create the radio spots. He sent me soundbites from the play, and my job was to craft them into a compelling story that would drive ticket sales.

We worked tirelessly, refining the script again and again until we had a commercial that captured the production's excitement. From that moment on, I worked on all of David's plays — *What Goes Around Comes Around, His Woman, His Wife, Love in a Nick of Time, He Say She Say*—and we became lifelong friends. During this era, promoters capitalized on the Black play circuit's success, with some productions grossing over a million dollars in just a two-week run per city.

In 1995, I got a call from Walter Latham. He had an idea for a comedy tour featuring the biggest names in Black comedy, filling arenas instead of theaters. My job was to capture the funniest soundbites from each comedian and create a campaign that made people feel like they *had* to be there. The lineup was Cedric the Entertainer, Bernie Mac, D.L. Hughley, and Steve Harvey. The show was called *The Kings of Comedy*. Not only did I voice the radio campaign, but I was also the voice heard in the show, introducing Steve Harvey as the host.

Another one of my longtime clients and friends was Ricky Walker, who co-created the hit stage play *A Good Man Is Hard to Find*, which was wildly successful in the '90s. When that run ended, Ricky had another vision: an all-Black circus. I'll admit, at first, I doubted it. Where was he going to find Black circus performers with elephants, tigers, acrobats, and all the other elements? But Ricky was relentless. He traveled the world, assembling an extraordinary cast. In 1994, *The UniverSoul Circus* debuted, and it was spectacular.

This shows that when a person has a vision, other people's doubts cannot stop what God has put in their heart to achieve. When I witnessed the circus for the first time, my mouth dropped in amazement. Ricky did it! And I was honored that Voice Over Productions had the opportunity to produce the first radio commercials for its debut tour.

In the late '90s, a Dallas promoter named Arthur Primas hired me to do the radio campaign for a play called *I Know I've Been Changed*. Like so many projects, it was always a challenge turning nothing into something, no soundbites, nothing. But as always, we made it work. I built the commercial around a gospel classic, "Lord, I Know I've Been Changed" by LaShun Pace. The powerful vocals played in the background while I delivered the script: "Don't miss the stage play that will have you shouting in the aisles, *I Know I've Been Changed*." The playwright behind the script insisted that his name be branded before the title. And so, we added the name Tyler Perry. That was the beginning of a relationship that lasted for years, with my voice narrating every one of his plays as he rose to become the most successful playwright in the business. His unique twist, playing the character of Madea, a sassy, outspoken grandmother, cemented his legacy in Black theater history.

Looking back, this was a season of tremendous growth, not just in business but in faith, family, and vision. God was taking me places I never expected, and I was just holding on for the ride.

Things God spoke to me:

*"Gerald, keep spending time with me, trust me.
I have already planned everything out for you and Karen.
I love both of you so much.
My word backs up everything I'm saying to you.
Know that I'm with you. You can trust me, Gerald.
You are under my great hand of protection.
This is where I need my people right here.
You know my voice, Gerald.
Continue to walk in my ways in this place.
Be not anxious for anything.
Know that I'm taking care of all of your needs.
Stay here for a while in my presence.
I'm doing some things on your behalf now.
The things I have for you are bigger than you could ever imagine.
Let my presence be with you throughout this day and every day.
I am with you, guiding you as you make these decisions.
Tell others that I want them to spend some real time with me."*

Chapter Thirteen

OUR BLACK ENTERTAINMENT

Many pivotal changes happened from 1996 to 1997. Karen and I had been dating off and on for the past year, mostly due to my indecisiveness. Karen was tired of just dating and ready for marriage, while I remained on the fence. To those of you who may be in this situation, it's not fair to either person to be put on hold like this. A commitment must be made sooner or later; if not, you have to let that person go so God can bring the right person into their lives.

Since I wasn't sure if Karen was the right person for me, I decided to break up with her. Needless to say, she was very disappointed. By then, she had moved into her own apartment in River Place, so occasionally bumping into her in the parking lot or hallways felt uncomfortable. We remained polite to each other with a quick hello before moving on. Sometimes when we crossed paths, I wondered what she really thought!

After we broke up, I didn't date much. Instead, I spent more time with my kids, who were now 15 and 13, and found myself praying more than ever before. My church held morning prayer at its Redford location from 6 am to 7 am, Monday through Friday. The Redford location was quite a drive from River Place downtown, about a half hour each way, but every morning I felt it was worth the effort. We gathered for corporate prayer, lifting up the president of the United States, government officials, local leaders, our church, and many other concerns. We also had time to pray for our personal lives. It was here that I developed the gift of praying in the spirit, or in tongues.

There was always something special about praying in the spirit, which sometimes ushered in God's presence, making the time and effort worthwhile. 1 Corinthians 14:2 and 14:4 highlight that speaking in tongues is directed toward God, not people, and edifies the speaker. Jude 1:20 says, "But you, dear friends, by building yourselves up in your most holy faith and praying in the Holy Spirit." Praying in the spirit gave me the sense that I was communicating with God in a higher, unique way that pleased him, allowing him to accomplish his purposes in my life through these prayers. I learned many mysteries about my future would be revealed during this time spent praying in the spirit.

Several months later, after consistently attending morning prayer, something happened that I had never experienced before: I heard the audible voice of God. Usually, He speaks to us through our inner spirit and, of course, through His Word. But hearing God through an audible voice is rare for most people and doesn't happen often. I read in Kenneth E. Hagin's book, *How to Be Led by the Spirit of God*, "When God moves in a more spectacular way by speaking in what seems to be an audible voice, it must be really important. If He had not spoken so spectacularly, we might not stay steady on what He spoke to us about."

As I sat in the pew at morning prayer with my Bible open to Hebrews 6:12, "That ye be not slothful, but followers of them who through faith and patience inherit the promises," I heard a voice as if someone was sitting right behind me. The voice spoke those exact words from the scripture, followed by, "You are to marry Karen at the appropriate time."

Immediately, I turned around because the voice seemed so close, as if a person was right behind me speaking, but when I turned around, no one was there. Honestly, I was confused about what I heard, yet it seemed so real and clear that I couldn't ignore it. I wanted to know who and what was speaking to me. I arranged several meetings with ministers on the church staff to help me understand what I had heard and experienced.

In one meeting with Pastor Ron Prichard, he confirmed that it could have very well been God speaking to me. My concern was whether it could be the enemy. After several counseling sessions, I came to the conclusion that it was up to me to decide if this was God speaking to me or not.

What happened that day at morning prayer was on my mind every day. It would be the first thing I thought about when I woke up and the last thing I thought about before I went to bed. It was that strong. Months and months went by, and finally, I decided to step out in faith and believe that this was God speaking to me. The more I meditated on the scripture He spoke to me, Hebrews 6:12, "That ye be not slothful, but followers of them who through faith and patience inherit the promises," the more it made sense that God was telling me not to be lazy in my faith, to continue being diligent in seeking Him, and that just like others who received His promises, so would I. But the caveat to that was I was to marry Karen. Why were the two connected? What did she have to do with the promises? I have surely learned that the person you marry can have a lot to do with the direction of your life for many different reasons.

Now that I had accepted it was the Lord speaking to me, how do I go back to Karen after I broke off the relationship with her? It had been almost a year! Would she still be interested in me? Or maybe she had started dating someone else! How do I even explain what had happened? Would she say, "You better get out of my face! I don't believe you have the nerve to ask me out again after what you did!" All of these things were going through my mind, but I kept reliving that moment when God spoke to me. Therefore, I had to do it! I had to go to her and see! Another step of faith.

I finally got up the nerve to call Karen. Of course, she immediately recognized my voice.

"Hey Gerald."

I said, "I was wondering if we could go out to dinner or something tomorrow night."

There was a slight pause from Karen, and I thought, "Uh oh, this is where she's going to give me a piece of her mind."

Instead, she said, "Well, tomorrow night's not good. I have a show with *Jammin' on the Groove* at Legends. Why don't you join me there?"

I agreed. What a sigh of relief!

We met the next night, and Karen was looking beautiful as always. But now I was looking at her in a different way. I knew God had a plan for both of us. I also realized this was different from a worldly approach to relationships, with just lustful physical attraction, which is not enough to sustain a long, happy marriage. I was ready to begin a journey of understanding how God sees marriage and what He expects from both of us.

After a few months of reuniting, I told Karen about my experience at morning prayer and how God had spoken to me. She was amazed to hear the story and excited because she had also been told to let me go, and if I was the man for her life, I would come back. A few weeks after that, I took her up to the lake where we had spent many summers with the kids and asked her to marry me. Of course, without hesitation, she said yes!

As members of Word of Faith Church, we took the premarital course recommended by the church, one of the best decisions any couple can make before marriage. Marriage counseling helped us align on money, children, discipline, our future, and most importantly, spiritual values. It really opened our eyes to understand what we were getting into.

One year later, Karen and I got married in Orlando, Florida, at Disney World with just us and the kids in a small ceremony, followed by a honeymoon for Karen and me in the Bahamas. I know this isn't your typical love story, but to have God speak to you about who your mate should be is truly a blessing. Also, just because God spoke to you about your mate doesn't mean things will always be perfect. Marriage takes work on both sides. But because we knew that God had spoken about our union as husband and wife, it would always be the glue that kept us together. The years ahead would prove to be a godly commitment, not just for us but for our entire family.

That same year, Karen and I bought our first home on Oak Drive in Detroit, a beautiful Spanish stucco house with huge cathedral ceilings. I absolutely loved this beautiful house in the same neighborhood where I grew up, but more than that, I loved the home we had built together. While Karen continued her job at the Music Hall Center for the Performing Arts downtown, I focused on growing Voice Over Productions. With some calls and promises, I relocated to a suite at my alma mater, the Spec Howard School of Broadcasting.

My suite, located on the second floor above the school, featured three beautifully designed radio production rooms and an outer office area, all newly remodeled to my specifications. Finally, a real studio in an office building, not an apartment. In this space I was able to employ more staff, expand my recording equipment, and had the room to take on advertising agencies for work. I finally felt like I had reached the pinnacle of where I dreamed Voice Over Productions would always be. This was part of the plan God had for my business.

As expected, the demands of running the business became even greater. I developed a daily routine of prayer and meditation in the morning, followed by breakfast. By 9 or 10 am, I was in the studio creating the several radio commercials that had been ordered. By 2:30

pm, it was time to head to the radio station for my shift as the afternoon drive host on WMXD MIX 92.3 from 3 to 7 pm. In many instances, I barely made it to the station on time. I remember the receptionist, Sheila, joking about it as I dashed through the door at 2:58, just in time to start my shift.

"Watch out, move out of the way! Here he comes!" Sheila would shout as I ran into the studio just in time to say, "WMXD MIX 92.3 Detroit."

This routine continued until one day, during a staff meeting with Program Director Monica Starr and the rest of the on-air team, Monica emphasized the importance of giving 120% to our on-air performances. She also required that we arrive an hour before our shifts for prep time. As I sat there at the back of the staff meeting, I thought to myself, *"How can I do that?"* My schedule was already too packed, and between balancing Voice Over Productions, taking calls with clients even while on the air, and ensuring my staff kept the work going, there was hardly any time left for me to arrive at the station one hour prior to my shift. Right then, I believe the Lord spoke to me that it was time to leave my radio job. A clear revelation also hit me as I thought over the matter: *"How would you feel if your employees were running their own businesses on your dime?"* That was all the confirmation I needed to go full-time into my own business.

Over the years, many people have asked me, "How do you start your own business? When do you quit your job?" My advice: start your business while still employed and balance both until your business is stable enough to sustain your living income.

After the staff meeting, I walked straight into Monica's office. "Hey Monica, can I talk to you for a moment?"

"Sure, Gerald, what can I do for you?" she asked.

I answered frankly. "I heard what you said about giving the station 120%, but my business is doing so well that I think it's time for me to resign."

Right then and there, I let go of an $82,000 salary. However, I had another idea. I asked Monica, "What about letting me do a part-time shift on Saturday nights? If you allow me to play what I want, I could make this a popular show."

She loved the idea. And so, *Saturday Night Live* was born. The show ran every Saturday from 7 pm to midnight on WMXD Mix 92.3. I was paid 50 dollars a show. After working for so many radio stations and following music selections dictated by program directors, I was finally given the freedom to program my own show. This was a rare opportunity for a DJ, and I knew it was nothing but the favor of God. I was determined to make the most of it. The oldies show, hosted by yours truly, went on to become one of the highest-rated shows on Detroit radio.

In 1999, my son Jaz graduated from high school and entered Dillard University in New Orleans. I'll never forget the long ride down south to drop him off at college, getting him set up in his dorm room on campus and giving him that last father and son talk on a bench outside his dorm room. He was a pretty independent thinker. There was no doubt in my mind that he would be okay. In these moments you hope that everything you taught your kids pays off and they remember the advice you gave them and use it wisely. With boys it's a little different. You have taught them survival skills, and a few hard knocks won't hurt them but only make them stronger. With that being said, I was comfortable with leaving him there and expected him to be able to make it and figure it out. With a few twists and turns and hard lessons learned here and there, he made it through the obstacles.

A year later, Alana enrolled at Howard University in D.C. She was very smart and had planned to major in chemical engineering, which she did very well. Leaving her for the first time on campus was a little different. But we also believed that we had prepared her the best we could. The Bible says, "Train up a child in the way they should go." This was more difficult for Karen, leaving her only child on this campus that seemed very busy! We stayed in D.C. for about a week before Alana finally said, "Mom, I'm going to be okay. You can leave now."

Brandy, unsure about her next steps after high school, decided to stay home. After discussing her options, I suggested she study video editing at Spec Howard School of Broadcasting, which was conveniently located in the same building as my business. She agreed, and after graduating, she became my first video editor. This was how Voice Over Productions evolved into a one-stop shop for TV and radio production. The system we developed was simple: I created the audio, and Brandy followed my lead to create the video. Unlike most production companies, where video editors also create audio, we had a seamless father-daughter system that continues to this day.

By 2003, Voice Over Productions (VOP) had become a full-service production company for TV and radio. We landed a major client, AEG Live, through Jeff Sharpe, who had become head of Urban Concerts. With Billy Sparks as a consultant, we handled promotional tours for Usher, Janet Jackson, Earth, Wind & Fire, Charlie Wilson, Stevie Wonder, Prince, Babyface, Jeffrey Osborne, Keith Sweat, Kem, and many more.

While VOP thrived, I continued my little Saturday night R&B oldies show on WMXD, making just $50 per show. The money didn't matter; I was more interested in staying connected with my radio audience and the station where I had worked for 25 years. One night, while fooling around on the air, I asked, "What if we put Michael Jackson up against Prince in a musical battle? Who do you think would win?" The phone lines lit up with strong opinions! Realizing the audience's excitement, I decided to play their songs back-to-back and let the listeners vote. This was how the House Party Battle of the Old School was born.

Each week, we featured a combination of two or three different artists battling in a two-hour showdown. The show's popularity skyrocketed. It felt like throwing a party every weekend, playing everyone's favorite records, and bringing back their fondest memories.

The show's success led us to syndication, meaning my show would play on several other stations simultaneously each weekend. I started out with affiliates WDKX in Rochester, NY, Star 99.7 in Charleston, NC, WDZZ in Flint, MI, and KCEP in Las Vegas, NV. Even though I had no sponsors and was providing the show for free, I knew it had potential. Once we reached fifteen stations, I approached Superadio, a syndication company in New York, and we struck a deal. They helped expand the show to eighteen stations, but even with a few advertisers, it struggled financially.

In fact, I was losing money because I had to pay my producer, Lance, and my co-hosts, Theresa and Andre. Many times, I considered shutting it down because it just wasn't making any sense. Sense or cents! I would often ask myself, "Why am I paying to be on the radio? Everybody is getting paid but me!" This went on for years. But something inside was saying, "Keep going. One day it's going to pay off." I would be reminded of a scripture in Jeremiah 29:11: "For I know the thoughts that I think toward you, saith the LORD, thoughts of peace, and not of evil, to give you an expected end."

Even though I went through days of doubt, I knew God had planned this. But I had to wait on Him. This would be a lesson I would have to learn over and over: wait and trust God.

Slowly, the checks started coming in. It would take years, but eventually, the show turned profitable. I went from 10 to 33 stations in 10 years! Looking back, I see how faith, persistence, and divine favor played a role in every step of my journey.

Things God spoke to me:

"Faith makes prayer work.
Wait on me, Gerald, for I have something greater than
you could imagine.
Continue to allow me to use you, Gerald.
People will see the great blessings in your life.
Remember to come to me when you feel anxiety, fear,
and frustration.
Come to me, Gerald.
This is where you find comfort and peace.
I am always here for you.
This secret place of refuge.
Read my word; it is true for you. It can stand the test
of time.
You will know what to say and pray as you stay in
my presence.
You will feel the love that comes from me when you pray.
Trust me as my protection surrounds you and
your family.
Do you see the blessing?
(Yes, I see it, Lord, and I thank you for what you have
done in my life.
Thank you, Father.)"

Chapter Fourteen

THE FUTURE OF NOW

One of my biggest clients was North American Entertainment Group, headed by Brian Alden. They were highly successful in producing plays in the late '90s and 2000s. Brian also produced numerous comedy shows and concerts, sometimes doing as many as one hundred shows a year.

We first met in the '90s, when he and his partner, Marvin Webster, were doing plays. A few were written by a faith-filled couple named Derrick and Celestine Brinkley. Often, they would come to the studio, and we would spend hours recording sound bites for their various plays. These snippets were used in radio spots to give the audience a sense of the story.

One day, while we were gathered in the office, Derrick's brother-in-law asked if he could pray for us. Of course, I said yes. Who would turn down a prayer? As he began to pray, he prophetically spoke over our company, Voice Over Productions, declaring that one day we would be producing major films with big-name actors. At the time, I thought it was an exaggeration. I had no desire to make movies and felt like he had no idea what he was talking about. It was the farthest thing from my mind.

Years passed, and we remained busy producing radio commercials for Brian Alden and his shows. In 2007, when he came to town to talk with some of the radio stations he had dealt with for years, he also made a visit to my studio, Voice Over Productions, which was located in the Spec Howard School of Broadcasting. Like most clients, most of my interactions and correspondence were over the phone or email, so this would be the first time I would see Brian in person.

I was quite surprised by his appearance. A salt-and-pepper-haired Jewish guy who looked very mild-mannered, quite different from the aggressive, hard, no-nonsense person I talked to on the phone, who was always straight to the point. In person, he seemed totally different, almost a different personality, which was much nicer, softer-spoken, and just a genuinely nice guy. We spent the entire day together as I took the time to escort him to the different radio stations where he had appointments.

By late afternoon, he mentioned that his son was also in town. His son, Peter, was playing hockey for UMass, and they were facing U of M in Ann Arbor. Of course, I said, "Yes, I'd be glad to take you." When we arrived, I was amazed to see the 10,000-seat arena completely sold out. It was my first time at a hockey game, and I quickly noticed I was the only black person in the entire arena. The fast pace of the game thrilled me, and unlike other sports, scoring was much more difficult. However, one thought kept nagging me. It was more of a question: where were the black people? There were none in the stands and certainly none playing on the ice.

This observation sparked an idea for a movie. I envisioned the beginning, imagined the middle, and visualized the end. The next day, I couldn't shake the idea. It consumed my thoughts. It's amazing how God places ideas in your heart, making you restless until they are fulfilled. And yes, what was prophesied to me a few years back by the man in my office, and that I didn't believe, was now coming to fruition. Can we trust something that has been prophesied over us? Most of the time, when it confirms something you already know, yes, you can run with it. But in this case, the man saw something in me that I didn't see in myself, which has been part of the story of my life, where people saw more potential in me than I could see at the time. But this time, after going to the hockey game, God himself confirmed what I had heard and put the burning desire in my heart to write, giving me the idea for the story.

Even though I had no experience writing screenplays, I did my best to create an outline, list characters, and jot down the story on a notepad. As I developed the script further, I acquired Final Draft screenwriting software and attended a two-day workshop taught by a Hollywood producer. Night after night, week after week, I dedicated my evenings to refining the script, which I called *Black Ice*. The process reminded me of when I worked in radio and God placed it on my heart to leave my job and start my own business. It was another moment of transition, but this time, it would take years of preparation.

After four years of working on the script, I began sharing it with a few people. Some loved the concept, but the story still needed work. I sent it to my friend Dave Talbert, who had experience producing top-rated movies. Dave passed it along to his agent at CAA (Creative Artists Agency) for an evaluation. The report came back with a page full of big red zeros. It was pretty discouraging to see so much disapproval for my work. I also received many disparaging notes from various people, but I reminded myself that these were just opinions. I took what I liked from each piece of feedback and made improvements. This process continued for several more years.

Yet, despite all my efforts, I still couldn't get people to read the script or invest in it, but I was determined to never give up. It would have been nice if I could have worked on my writing skills and script full-time. I would have progressed much faster. But I had paying clients and employees who were depending on me. So the job at Voice Over Productions had to be done, but that burning desire to write would always be inflamed in my heart, calling to me. It seemed like, for a while, I was putting it off, but we have to make a living.

My advice to you, if you see yourself in the same situation with an opportunity to grow into your dream, don't let the flame dwindle. Keep it lit by doing what you can when you can. If it means in your free time, when you get off work, instead of just sitting around watching TV, dedicate that time to putting work into your dream. It may not happen as fast as you want, but you are doing something to keep it alive and the fire burning.

In June of 2008, my daughter Brandy married her longtime boyfriend, Duasean Mitchell. They had known each other since their teenage years, and now they were committing their lives to one another.

I'll never forget the first time I met Duasean. He was just 17, and it was at a backyard birthday party Karen and I hosted for Alana. Duasean showed up with his brother and a few friends. Everything was going well—until a fight broke out in the street. Duasean and his crew jumped up, ready to get involved. To this day, I'm still not sure how it ended, but that was my very first impression of this young man who had taken an interest in my daughter.

What I didn't know then—but would come to see—was that Duasean had a powerful calling on his life. His father and family were deeply rooted in ministry, and it wasn't long before Duasean answered God's call, dedicating his life fully to the Lord. Brandy followed his lead, and together they became a couple on fire for God. I couldn't have been more proud.

Their wedding was beautiful—a warm summer day in downtown Detroit. I'll never forget walking my little girl down the aisle, tears streaming as I handed her over to the man she loved. Brandy looked stunning in her gown, and Duasean stood there patiently, waiting for his bride. In that moment, I couldn't help but think, "*How did we get here so fast?* My little girl had grown into a beautiful young woman, ready to begin a new chapter."

During the reception, I had the chance to speak—and surprise the guests with something unforgettable. My friend Altero Shelton, a well-known impressionist around the city, had agreed to perform his spot-on Stevie Wonder impersonation. I built up the suspense, teasing the crowd: "Alright, ladies and gentlemen, get ready for a very special guest... he's doing me a favor tonight, and you're in for a treat. Are you ready?"

The room erupted: "Yeah!"

When Altero walked out, dressed exactly like Stevie—braids, shades, the signature smile—people went crazy. They pulled out their phones, calling friends: "*You won't believe this... Stevie Wonder is here!*" Jamella, a program director from the radio station, made it look official by escorting him to the piano in the center of the room. When Altero began playing "My Cherie Amour," the room was electric. People were convinced it was Stevie himself! Eventually, after a few songs, I revealed the truth—it was Altero, the city's best impressionist. The crowd erupted with laughter and applause. To this day, people still talk about that moment.

Brandy and Duasean have since become co-pastors at his father's church and, most recently, have been ordained as lead pastors. I couldn't be prouder of what God has done in their lives. They are fully committed to building the Kingdom and saving souls, and it humbles me to see how far they've come—from teenage sweethearts to powerful servants of God.

I constantly received calls and emails from people asking about the voice-over industry. I would hear, "Someone told me I had a nice voice. I was wondering if I could get into voice-overs." Actually, that's a good question. At the time, there weren't many classes you could find in schools or colleges or even online about this art form. For me, it was part of the job as a radio announcer. But for the average person who wanted to do something with this gift of a nice voice, why not try to find a way to use it and make a few extra dollars?

So Randy Z, an instructor at Spec Howard, and I created a voice-over class that we taught once a month for two consecutive Saturdays from Voice Over Productions. Every month, we trained eight to twelve students. The first week focused on techniques, script reading, union vs. non-union jobs, breathing techniques, and auditions. Each student received scripts as homework. The following week, we recorded their individual demos, which consisted of ads from our collection of scripts or from ones they created on their own.

I always taught them there were many styles of voice-overs. First, the announcer's voice-over. Usually, the voices and styles that fit this category are like mine, the big radio voice heard on concert promos, TV promos, movie trailers, and more. At the time I was teaching this class, one of the biggest voices in the industry was a guy named Don LaFontaine. He became identified with the phrase "In a world...," used in so many movie trailers that it became a humorous catchphrase. Widely known in the film industry, the man whose nicknames included "Thunder Throat," "The Voice of God," and "The King of Movie Trailers" became known to a wider audience through commercials for GEICO insurance and the Mega Millions lottery game.

Don became one of the most recognized voices in the industry, making millions with his pipes. I heard that he was so sought after by studios and ad agencies that in his contract, he had to be picked up in a stretch limo and driven to the recording studio if he was hired.

The other style is character voices. Your character voices are the animated voices you hear in cartoons, video games, and more. This is a huge industry! Most of the voices you hear in animation these days are Hollywood stars who are making a ton of money by being themselves while portraying these animated characters. But nevertheless, there are still plenty of jobs in animation for character voices, whether you are a star or not. It's funny how many people would call me on the phone to inquire about voice-overs and go into character voice with a quick audition to show me their talent, even when I didn't ask! Character voices could also mean that you can do a good impersonation of a famous person like Donald Trump, Denzel Washington, Eddie Murphy, Mike Tyson, Halle Berry, or anyone with a recognizable voice who is famous. The only problem with this is that it has to be very good. There's nothing worse than a bad impersonation.

Another popular style of character voice-over we talked about in the class was the regular, everyday voice. This seemed to fit most of our students. Agencies are looking for everyday people to play everyday people, like mothers, fathers, sisters, brothers, store clerks, etc. You get the drift, the everyday lives of people doing everyday things in commercials. Is this starting to sound like acting? Well, it is. It's called voice acting. The art of voice-over is to read without sounding like you're reading. To take a script of words on a page and bring them to life. I would always tell the students to be themselves when reading these scripts. Here is an example of the kinds of scripts we handed out. Most of these scripts were actual jobs I would audition for.

Script Sample 1

Leaky-boil-tested :15 AVO: Only Glad trash bags with LeakGuard actually absorb liquids. So they're not only leak-tested... **AVO:** They're... Brought-half-the-ocean-to-the-seafood-boil-tested. **DAD:** Who's ready for round 2? **AVO:** New Glad with LeakGuard absorbs liquids.

All-by-himself-tested :15 AVO: Only Glad trash bags are odor-tested, leak-tested, rip-tested... **AVO:** And... Noah-asked-to-do-it-alllllll-by-himself tested. **AVO:** So you all can relax on trash day.

Distracted-teen-tested :15 AVO: Only Glad with LeakGuard trashbags absorb liquids. So they're not only leak-tested... AVO: They're... Mom's-new-white-suede-bench-tested. AVO: New Glad with LeakGuard absorbs liquids.

Script Sample 2

This Is Home :30

GIRL: *SING-SONGY* WALT DISNEY WORLD! YOU'RE MY WORLD! DAD: *CHUCKLES* OH, YOU CAME TO PLAY, HUH?

GIRL: WE HAD THE BEST DAY, NO BEST WEEK EVER, DAD! I HUGGED MICKEY MOUSE...RODE MICKEY AND MINNIE'S RUNAWAY RAILWAY, ATE MICKEY ICE CREAM BARS, MICKEY PRETZELS, MICKEY WAFFLES.

DAD: MICKEY MICKEY MICKEY. I THOUGHT *I* WAS YOUR FAVORITE? *HE TEASES* GIRL: *LAUGHING* STAAAHP, DAD. DAD: WELL, AFTER THE FIREWORKS, WE CAN GO HOME. GIRL: HOME? NOOOO...

DAD: YOU DON'T WANT TO GO OUR YACHT CLUB RESORT-HOME?

GIRL: OHHHHHH... THAT HOME!

DAD: YES GOOFY GIRL! AND WE CAN PLAY AGAIN TOMORROW.

AVO: READY TO PLAY? VISIT DISNEY WORLD [DOT] COM [BACKSLASH] CAME TO PLAY.

Living the Fantasy :15

RAVEN: WALT DISNEY WORLD KNOWS HOW TO DO A PARADE! EVERYBODY'S FEELING ME. FREYA: YOU? WE CAME TO PLAY, REMEMBER?

RAVEN: WATCH. *SPEAKING OFF TO THE CHARACTERS* MINNIE MOUSE! LOVE THOSE YELLOW SHOES! RAPUNZEL! YES GIRL! THE HAIR IS

GIVING! RAVEN: SEE? *SHE LAUGHS, A LITTLE HAUGHTY*
FREYA: *LAUGHS WITH HER* **GIRL, CHILL. THERE'S ENOUGH MAGIC FOR EVERYBODY. AVO: READY TO PLAY? VISIT DISNEY WORLD [DOT] COM [BACKSLASH] CAME TO PLAY.**

As we recorded the demos, I spent about an hour in the studio making sure they nailed their reads, adding variety in inflection, tone, and tempo, then chose the right background music for each commercial. The demos would be about 60 seconds long, all that's needed for a demo. Usually, a talent agency can tell if the person has what it takes in the first 20 seconds. Each student walked away with a CD of their demo and was encouraged to send it to production houses and agencies, hoping to be signed and added to their roster of talent.

Just because you get signed to an agency does not mean you automatically get work and get paid. You have to go through the process of auditioning for jobs. I informed the students to be prepared to get turned down. But you have to keep auditioning again and again until you get hired. We have to remember that it's a competitive field, just like acting. Listen to the many voices you hear on the radio, TV spots, automated message systems, video games, tutorial videos, audiobooks, and the list just goes on and on. There are hundreds and hundreds of VO jobs out there. They just need to know who you are and hear your skills. So, you have to get your demos out there, network, and let people know that you do this.

I also encouraged my students to do some VO work for free, such as voicemail messages for friends, church announcements, or wherever a recorded voice is needed. If you've ever wondered how many voice-over jobs are out there, just start paying attention to the many voice-overs you hear throughout everyday life: on the radio, TV, automated phone recordings, voicemail, on your computer, phone apps, tutorials, Siri,

Alexa, and your car. When you think about it, the list just goes on and on.

Now that you have your demo tape, you are in the business of voice-overs. So, create a voice-over company with a website and business cards that advertise your home studio and your readiness to do voice-overs. Treat it as a legitimate business. Having a home studio is important and easy these days with a laptop, a USB mic, and some simple recording software. You can record at home. Just make sure the audio is clean by recording in a quiet place in your home, and also make sure there is no distortion in your mic or software. Once you have a studio, practice as much as you can, reading different scripts and auditioning as much as you possibly can. Take advanced VO classes and try to improve with an even better demo.

I gave this advice to many who took the class, and some have gone on to become successful voice-over artists. Some I have used and hired for voice-over work on various projects. Last, if this is something you're interested in, give it your best shot and go for it! You never know, you might get that one job where your voice becomes the brand for that product or event. Look at Flo for Progressive Insurance or the voice of the gecko for Geico Insurance. They have become voices that we have grown to love and remember.

For almost 10 years, I was the voice of a local clothing store in Metro Detroit that consistently advertised on TV and radio. The owner only wanted my voice, which proved to brand his name and store. I would average three to five commercials a week, which added up to a nice piece of change! For those of you who lived in Metro Detroit, I'm sure you remember the clothing store, Mr. Alan's! The voice you heard for many years doing the price points of "29 or 2 for 50" was me!

In 2009, during the economic crash, it seemed like business just came to a halt for us. Concerts were almost nonexistent as promoters withdrew from booking shows. This was 90 percent of our business. I had no choice but to move out of the expensive $3,000-a-month suite at Spec Howard School of Broadcasting and relocate the business to my home. My office manager, Martina King, and I transformed the lower level into a studio with a video suite, audio recording room, and accounting office.

I remember struggling to pay rent and salaries, but somehow, we managed to survive. At one point, my business account had only $2.35! Moments like these truly test your faith, but I held onto God's promise that He would supply all my needs. A silver lining of working from home was spending more time with my daughter Brandy, who now had two children, Tandie and Cooper.

Brandy often brought the kids to work, and this allowed me to watch my grandchildren grow. Tandie, in particular, loved the microphone. At just three years old, we recorded her voice in the studio, and she loved hearing herself on playback. From ages three to eight, we featured her voice on special promos for her birthday parties, inviting friends and family. She'd been doing voice-over work since she was six, and by 13, she was already a pro with ads running on radio and TV. It all started with that home studio.

Meanwhile, Cooper had a passion for dinosaurs, but he also displayed artistic and musical talent. Interestingly enough, he now produces movies featuring his dinosaurs.

My home office was becoming a comfortable place to work, especially for me, since I could work long hours without worrying about the commute. My employees consisted of Martina King for accounting, Brandy Mitchell for video editing, and Nina Wiggins for traffic. I also used Karl Jackson as a part-time subcontractor for video editing and videography, and Mike McDaniels for voice-overs. For a while, my concern was whether or not my clients would take us seriously if we were considered a home-based business, but as it turned out, it didn't matter as long as the work was good.

Political spots were always a big part of business, having done radio spots for Dennis Archer for mayor, Kwame Kilpatrick, several city council members, the NAACP, and many more. So when political season rolled around, right out of my basement, we continued to provide quality work. Clients like Dave Bing, who was running for mayor, didn't mind coming to my house to record.

One day, while in my office, I received a call from my friend Robert Shumake. He asked if I could help a friend, Marcus Murray, produce a motivational CD. Of course, I agreed. Marcus and I hit it off immediately, and after a few recording sessions, his project was complete. His voice carried confidence, and his message was filled with affirmation and encouragement. After we completed the project, Marcus and I remained close friends. I always knew there was something more than just a business relationship. a friendship that would last a lifetime.

One morning during prayer, the Lord spoke to me about buying him a suit. It seemed strange, but I never doubted God's instructions. I immediately called Marcus and asked him to meet me at The Broadway, a fine menswear store in Detroit. When I explained that God had placed it on my heart to bless him with a suit, he accepted the gift. I believe he still has it to this day. Looking back, I realize God was establishing a covenant between us.

The journey of life requires a running partner, someone who encourages you when you feel like quitting. As the Bible says, "Iron sharpens iron," and I thank God for bringing Marcus Murray into my life.

A lot of good things came out of working out of my basement. It was a humbling experience as I had to decrease in order to increase. Sometimes, the circumstances in life have a way of shaping your direction. But we must always remember that God is still on the throne. And if you ask Him and acknowledge Him in all your ways, He will direct your paths. When He tells us to step down or take a step back, we must trust Him because it's for our own good.

Things God spoke to me:

"You listen to me. Here's the breakthrough right here.
People will see the results of your prayer time.
It will be evident. Stay humble, knowing that it is me.
You'll know exactly what to do when this
breakthrough comes.
It is here. Prepare yourself.
What has been holding back the real blessing has
been broken.
Because of your obedience and faithfulness, all shall see.
I have given you the power to get wealth.
To establish my covenant.
It will be evident that my blessing is on you.
Remember the words in Deuteronomy
that I have spoken over you and your family's life.
My favor covers you. I am here, Gerald, as always.
I put these desires in you, Gerald.
Trust me, Gerald. Walk in my ways, trusting me.
Many prayers of the righteous are being answered."

Chapter Fifteen

Faith & Good Fortunes

By 2013, things had stabilized. My son had built his own business, Adwater Media, serving clients in the automotive industry. In 2014, we decided to move out of my home office into a beautiful suite on Northwestern Highway, which became the headquarters for VOP and Adwater Media. Around this time, I signed with several voice-over talent agencies, including WME (William Morris Entertainment). Each week, I received scripts to audition for. As I mentioned, the only way to land jobs through the agency was to audition. Though I spent a lot of time auditioning, most of my work came through the clients I had established relationships with over the years.

After three years of auditions, I finally booked my first major job with WME, a movie trailer for Shaft, starring Samuel L. Jackson! This was a dream come true. I had always wanted to do movie trailers, and the pay was exactly what I had imagined, over $15,000 for just a short session.

Here's the script I voiced:

SHAFT - TV Gerald McBride VO Script

"*This Weekend Comes The Ultimate Father's Day Comedy*"
"The Perfect Blend Of Action And Humor."
"Woke And Funny."
"Shaft Brings It Again."
"Unapologetically Cool."
"Funniest Action-Packed Thriller Of The Summer."
"One of this Year's Must-See Films."
"Couldn't Stop Laughing."
Alt: See The Ultimate Father's Day Comedy*
"On June 14th."
"You Don't Have To Wear Black To Be The Man"
"Alt: Real Men Don't Wear Black"

My days were full of production and a busy office six days a week. Moreover, the radio show I ran had grown to more than 25 stations across the country. The Old School House Party was performing well in all markets, and it was still a lot of fun going into the studios on Saturday nights with Andre and Theresa. Our connection with the live audience made the show even more enjoyable, and the non-stop positive feedback kept things going. One of our more popular listeners was a caller who always introduced herself as "the one and only Rubee!" She was such a regular caller on the show that many of our listeners came to love her as a part of the show.

Rubee had a slur when she talked, a deliberate mimicry that made her character interesting. She would talk as if she had been drinking, though she always claimed she never drank. The listeners loved her as she reminded them of "that aunt in every family" who would say anything after a few drinks at the family reunion and who always gave funny but great advice.

Between the shows and VOP work, I always managed to carve out time to work on the script for *Black Ice*. As I wrote the lines for each character, I hired a ghostwriter to type them into Final Draft. I quickly found it was better to have someone to collaborate with and ask for help creating lines for a particular character. Whenever I needed help crafting dialogue for a female character, my female writing partner Dorthia provided insight into how a woman might respond in certain situations. Her feedback made a significant difference in bringing authenticity to the script.

After countless critiques and rewrites, the story finally started coming together. I continued seeking industry feedback, but no real interest came from Hollywood. Once again, I reached out to my friend Dave Talbert. Even though he was busy, he took the time to listen to my idea and thought it had real potential. It was always encouraging to get positive feedback, especially from someone in the business, but still, no deal came for the film.

In 2017, I discovered a deeper relationship with the Lord. My days had always begun with prayer, but now, as I spent more time in His presence, I began to experience Him in a way I never had before. If I could put it into words, it felt like a smooth, velvety sensation, an undeniable peace that surpassed all understanding. Suddenly, the things I had worried about seemed so small, almost insignificant. His presence became my reassurance, a powerful reminder of His love and protection. While many experience this in a church service, I learned how to tap into it daily during my quiet time. I noticed that it often took time to quiet my mind, shut out distractions, and focus on Him. But once I reached that place, I never wanted to leave. It became my "secret place" with the Most High. To make this a priority, I started waking up early. Before

Karen was awake and ready to chat, I'd retreat to my library, surrounded by the faith books I had collected over the years, to just sit in the presence of God.

My routine always began with praise and worship, simply thanking God for all He was doing in my life. I'd read Scriptures and continue studying a faith-filled book before praying in the Spirit. Some mornings, it took nearly an hour to clear my mind, but the reward was always worth it. As I prayed, I could sense His presence so clearly. In those moments, I would ask the Lord to speak to me, and when He did, I made sure to write it down, journaling daily. After all, this was the Creator of the universe, the Alpha and Omega, speaking. How could I not record His words? And thus, journaling became a part of my daily walk with Him, something I've been doing ever since.

It was interesting that writing down what God had said to me and writing a book or movie script always correlated with each other. The Holy Spirit is also playing a great part in the flow of the words. I could sense that God was giving me the desire to write more and more, and writing down what He spoke to me was part of the process of learning to become a writer.

God's words are always so encouraging, loving, and kind. He would always say to me, "Trust that you know my voice; trust that this is me speaking to you." As it is written in John 10:27-28: "My sheep hear my voice, and I know them, and they follow me: And I give unto them eternal life; and they shall never perish, neither shall any man pluck them out of my hand."

* * *

As 2018 rolled around, Voice Over Productions continued to thrive, and our syndicated radio show had expanded to 32 markets. People from all over the world were calling my mobile 1-800-SOULJAM request line to vote for their favorite artist. The show was filled with endorsements and growing stronger by the day.

That same year, I discovered an organization called Transformation Film Institute, a filmmaking workshop based in Dallas and led by Pastor Richard Polite. It was a seven-day intensive course held on an actual movie studio lot, complete with small villages for filming and biblical sets with cobblestone streets and clay houses.

Something in my spirit told me this was no coincidence. I knew deep down that this was a divine opportunity, one that could help shape the very calling God had placed on my heart: to make faith-based films that weren't just "churchy," but that carried real, honest, life-changing messages leading people to Christ.

When God calls you to do something, He doesn't always hand you the blueprint. Sometimes He gives you one faith step at a time. That's when obedience becomes your greatest act of worship. For me, that step was saying yes to learning, to stretching, to preparing for the vision He gave me.

I've learned that faith without preparation is just wishful thinking. If you truly believe God has called you to a purpose, then you must be willing to take the steps (attend the classes, find the workshops, connect with the mentors) that will equip you for the journey ahead.

> *"Commit to the Lord whatever you do, and He will establish your plans."*
> —Proverbs 16:3 (NIV)

God did, one step at a time.

I enrolled in June 2018, eager to gain insight into the filmmaking process. The workshop took place in a massive mansion on the studio grounds, where all 15 students stayed, slept, and ate together. Each day began with prayer, as Richard emphasized that making faith-based films was more than just a career; it was a calling. He reminded us to leave our egos at the door and focus on serving God through storytelling. Prayer time was a priority. He encouraged us, "If you are going to write and produce scripts, get before God and find out what He wants you to write about and get wisdom on how you are going to move forward with the project." This would be something I would always remember: getting God involved in every aspect of my project.

The first few days covered classroom instruction on camera equipment, lighting, lenses, shot variations, crew roles, directing, producing, and more. Later, we took on those roles ourselves to create a short film, which we screened on the final day. During the workshop, I had the opportunity to share my own script, the main reason I had attended.

One of the instructors, Ashlee Woolridge, asked if she could read it, and in excitement, I handed it over. After a few hours, she returned and said, "I love it! I want to help you get this done!" For the first time, it felt like a real door had opened for my film.

Even while on trips like this, I always found a way to maintain my quiet time with God. On the studio grounds, there was a breathtaking garden that resembled the Garden of Gethsemane. I took my Bible there, played worship music, and spent time in God's presence. Returning home, I felt equipped with the knowledge and connections to move forward.

Around that time, a young producer had created a modernized concept for *The Fresh Prince of Bel-Air* without having the rights to the show. He filmed a high-quality trailer, and the internet exploded with excitement. The buzz caught Will Smith's attention, leading to a deal for a rebooted sitcom by this upcoming producer. This inspired me! What if I created a compelling pitch trailer for *Black Ice* to attract investors for the project? I called Ashlee, and she loved the idea. We quickly began pre-production, casting actors for the short script I wrote specifically for the trailer. Arthur Cartwright was chosen for the lead role, along with four teenage boys as hockey players and a young Caucasian actress as the recreation supervisor. The Detroit Ice Dreams Hockey players also assisted with the production.

Ashlee flew in from Dallas, bringing a film crew led by Jordan Lanseig, who handled cinematography. In just two days, we completed filming, and within a few weeks, Jordan's editing resulted in a polished, professional trailer. It was generating excitement, but despite the buzz, I still struggled to secure a deal.

In early 2019, I received a call from Markus Seabrooks, the same prophet who had spoken over my life a decade earlier about making movies, and I hadn't believed him. But here I was trying my best to fulfill the calling on my life. This time, I was anxious to hear what he had to say. He affirmed that God had positioned me to help reclaim the entertainment industry for His glory. He explained that God had appointed me to help take over the movie industry mountain that the enemy had taken as a stronghold for so long. He assured me that people like me and others would rise up to make quality faith-based films that would do very well in Hollywood. He also urged me to remain in control of my projects and not allow anyone to alter the stories God had given me. He went on to say many other things about my future in this business. But this time, as he said these things, I knew that they were confirmations of what I already knew. This reassurance made me confident that I was on the right track, and it was time to move forward. This is how you recognize that a prophet's words are true: they confirm what you already know in your heart.

The conversation I had with the prophet Markus helped me further understand that God had given me an assignment, a purpose, a mission to carry out on His behalf. The purpose of the film went beyond making money; it would serve as a message of hope, perseverance, forgiveness, and trust in God.

Things God Spoke to Me:

"You are building my Kingdom.
I have prepared you for such a time as this.
You are in my perfect will, and I am so pleased with who you have become.
Continue to trust me. <u>This where I need so many to be.</u>
Quietly with me. In this secret place.
Not in bragging about how spiritual you are,
But abiding in this quiet place with me.
This is where I can speak to you- this intimate place with me.
I have so much to say to all of you.
I want you to trust me more.
Leave it up to me, and I will show you.
One day, you will thoroughly understand it all.
There is much for you to do here.
I've given you everything you need to accomplish what I have called you to do."
"Keep trusting me
Praying in the spirit
And all things will work together for good
Keep trusting me
You are in my perfect will
You have revelation knowledge of my word
The blessing is on you.
The blood is protecting you.
I am working on your behalf now."

Chapter Sixteen

✟

LOCKDOWN LESSONS & LEADINGS

In late 2019, Ashlee, Jordan, and I sent out countless proposals to potential investors. Our proposed budget for *Black Ice* was $2.5 million, and we got as far as getting a Texas millionaire to show great interest in the project. Just when we began to celebrate having finally secured a deal, he backed out. Shortly after, COVID-19 hit, bringing everything to a halt.

In February of 2020, my beloved sister, Julie, was attacked by the COVID virus and lost her life. She had pre-existing health problems, including a kidney issue, and her body simply wasn't able to fight off the COVID-19 virus. This was during the early months of the pandemic, and the country had not been shut down when Julie died. A month later, we would learn more about this devastating virus and come to understand that it was the cause of her very untimely death.

Julie was a single mom with one daughter, Chelsea, who was in her late 20s, and a granddaughter, Zola, age 7. They were devastated by Julie's death, as the three of them had spent their lives together for many years in Julie's small apartment.

Unfortunately, Chelsea had no relationship with her father; she neither knew his identity or his whereabouts—at a time in her life when his support would have meant the most. Once a very prominent architect, her father had fallen into drug addiction. Rumor had it that he was now living somewhere on the streets of Florida, homeless.

I did my best to help my niece navigate through this difficult time for all of us, reminding her to get closer to God, that He was the only one who could comfort her with a peace that passes all understanding. After losing my mother a few years back, I understood the spirit of grief, and if not dealt with, it could become overwhelming. Yes, grief is a normal thing for us to go through, but we must not let it linger too long. Some people take years to get over the loss of someone close in their lives. The fact is that life will end for all of us sooner or later, but we pray that if loved ones gave their life to Jesus, we will see them again in eternity.

COVID-19 was a period of time when a lot of us had to face the challenges of losing a friend or a loved one. But it would be a time when we learned to trust and depend on God more and more.

Because 2020 brought everything to a grinding halt, the entertainment industry was one of the worst-affected sectors. With 85% of VOP's business being from the concert industry, this had a huge effect on us. No voice-over work of any kind crossed my desk, and the bank account started to dwindle. The only thing keeping me afloat was the PPP loan I received. Who would have ever thought that something like this would happen? Here we were, all stuck in our homes, uncertain of our future, as we heard news of people losing their lives and loved ones.

As we were reminded of our faith, so many of us felt the spirit of fear take over the world like never before. Once again, my opportunity to spend time with God and get to know Him more intimately was the priority in my life. Sometimes I think this was part of His reason for allowing the pandemic to happen, so that we would draw our attention to Him. It certainly worked for me.

As the months went by, Karen and I began to venture out little by little to places like church, grocery stores, and small gatherings at our kids' houses. COVID changed all our lives. Things we took for granted we suddenly appreciated much more. Of course, this brought Karen and me closer together. Looking back, we had some fun times during this hiatus. I remember taking a fun, two-week road trip to see the country. We went from Myrtle Beach to Charleston, then to Savannah, and across to Ripley, Tennessee, where we spent a couple of days with my cousin Donna and her husband, Tommy.

Being in Ripley brought back many memories of my childhood, when my parents would take us there every spring to visit my Uncle Samuel, Aunt Dorothy, and my grandparents. This was the town where my father, Andrew McBride, was born. My cousin's and uncle's house sat far up on a 20-acre hill overlooking the neighborhood. It was a beautiful green pasture with cows roaming and grazing throughout the land. It looked like a postcard. During our stay, we would step out onto the patio, watch the hot southern sunrise, and I would share the history of our family and my childhood memories spent right there.

My uncle, who bought the property many years ago, was now a 95-year-old widower, sharp as ever, and still driving. He asked Karen and me to take a drive with him to see the Mississippi River. I said, "Sure, only if I drive!" My cousin Donna had told me he wasn't the greatest driver at his age, but they didn't have the heart to take away his freedom. Besides, it was a small town, and his trips were short.

Even so, a few times a week, he would drive to the river to reminisce. As I followed his directions down the country highway, Uncle Samuel explained all the landmarks of his childhood: where he grew up, where his house once stood, his swimming hole, and the great Mississippi River. What a beautiful sight they all were as Karen and I stood on a hill in awe of this massive river. I believe that day brought my Uncle Samuel great joy as he explained the qualities of the river and how his family moved from one side of it to the other, to Arkansas, so that he and his siblings could have a better education.

I believe one of the things that helps older people live longer and keep their minds sharp is allowing them to revisit places they grew up and talk about their life experiences. Uncle Samuel passed away right before his 100th birthday. I will never forget the many stories he shared, a wealth of history that was always intriguing to me. If you ever had an uncle who sat in a rocking chair on the front porch of a house down south where your parents grew up, this is exactly like my Uncle Sammy. One of the real purposes and motivations in writing this book is to let my children and children's children know who I am and who my ancestors were. It is my great hope that our story will inspire them. This would be our historical trip to the south, rediscovering our roots and heritage.

Just like Karen was learning more about my family, I learned more about hers. After leaving Ripley, we headed to Locust Hill, Mississippi, to visit Karen's family and discuss family business involving land that was inherited by Karen and the rest of the family. Locust Hill is actually in a small town called Woodville, Mississippi. The land belonged to Karen's great-grandfather, who willed the land to two of his female slaves. It was very rare for a slave master to leave property to two of his slaves, especially 800 acres. The property was split between the two ladies, Ella Mason and Francis Swaggert.

Interestingly, the plantation owner's family came from Virginia to claim what they believed was their inherited property, only to find it was too late. The property had already been put in the two ladies' names. It was an impressive thing that, after all these years, Karen's family has maintained the land and kept it within the family. Because of the two families and all the members involved, the ongoing battle to find the rightful heirs continues to this day.

* * *

In 2021, Karen and I decided to switch churches. This wasn't an easy decision. For 25 years, we attended one of the greatest ministries in the country, Word of Faith International Christian Center in Southfield, Michigan, under Bishop Keith Butler, whose teaching of the Word has always been amazing. At Word of Faith, I also had the opportunity to serve in the TV ministry as the voice of the weekly church announcements and the "Live Your Faith" TV broadcast. Karen and I always knew the importance of being planted in and part of a local church.

People need to understand that it is not always advisable to move from church to church or attend a church just because it is conveniently located close to home. Rather, what is important is understanding that God has planted you in a specific place for a reason, regardless of the location. *Where are you supposed to be? Can God speak to you through the man or woman of God He placed in your life?* These should be the main questions you ask before choosing a church. Many people leave their present church for various reasons, such as political views, offense at something the pastor said, overcrowding, lack of parking spaces, song selection, or even because the pastor didn't greet them personally. The list goes on and on. My point is, stay where God has placed you and respect the pastor as your shepherd. If you are supposed to leave, let it be because the Lord is leading you away for a specific reason.

There were many things in church that I didn't necessarily agree with, but that wasn't a reason for me to leave where God had planted me. Consistency in being part of the body of Christ and expecting to hear from God through the person in the pulpit is vital. I also learned that every place of worship needs our talents and gifts to function properly. Volunteering is essential, from parking lot attendants, greeters, ushers, and custodians to worship team members, choir singers, kids' ministry leaders, prayer teams, and media ministries. Everyone contributes to making the church the vibrant place it is meant to be.

Since COVID, online church has become a new way of attending services. While some have grown comfortable with this format, nothing compares to the atmosphere of being present in person, especially when the sanctuary is filled with the presence of God. Additionally, in-person attendance provides opportunities to fellowship with other believers and stay connected with the body of Christ.

Almost 20 years ago, as I was leaving a service at Word of Faith, a fellow member, Claude, walked up to me and handed me a book. He said, "Gerald, I have a book I want to give you." The book was called *Produced by Faith* by DeVon Franklin, which detailed his journey in making faith-based movies. At the time, I had no desire or thoughts of making a movie. I wondered why Claude had given me this book, since I had never spoken to him about filmmaking. However, a few years later, that would all change when God placed a deep desire and a movie idea on my heart. Looking back, I see that God had already begun preparing me by having Claude give me this book. Needless to say, the book was incredibly inspiring. Had I not been in church or watching online, I would never have run into Claude, who was part of the inspiration for my filmmaking journey.

In 2021, Karen and I attended an anniversary party for Pastor Dominic Russo and his wife, Pastor Amie, at Oakland Church in Rochester, Michigan. It was a beautiful celebration at a nearby golf resort, packed with family and friends. Karen and I had a wonderful time fellowshipping with their family and church members. As the mic was passed around, we heard many testimonies about this amazing couple and how they had blessed so many people. It was evident that they had a genuine love for both God and people. They were well-respected and very approachable, as many gathered around them to offer congratulations. Karen and I truly enjoyed ourselves and met so many wonderful people that night.

On our way home, Karen told me, "You know, I really enjoyed myself tonight. I met some really nice ladies, and I think this is the kind of church we should belong to."

I was surprised by her comment and replied, "Why would we leave our church? We are receiving some of the best teaching ever through Word of Faith and Bishop Keith Butler. There's no reason for us to leave. Absolutely not!"

Karen was calm as she said, "Well, I think it is time for us to leave. We should pray about it."

To be quite honest, I didn't see any reason to pray about it. We had been part of one of the nation's greatest ministries. People don't just leave a church where the Word is preached so strongly.

The next day, during my prayer time, I sought the Lord about whether we should leave our church of 25 years and join Oakland Church. Spending time with God consistently had always been part of my daily routine, and through prayer, I expected to hear from Him. This was one of those decisions that required much prayer. The bigger the decision, the more prayer is needed. As I expected, God spoke to me—but not in the way I thought He would. To my surprise, He said clearly, "You have been at Word of Faith receiving all the Word and knowledge, but you haven't done anything with it. Yes, I do want you to attend Oakland Church."

Things God spoke to me:

"Stay focused on what I have called you to do.
Pray and walk in love, be consistent and confident in who you are in me.
Walk by the spirit no matter what.
I'm here, Gerald. There is a hedge of protection around you.
Share the declarations of walking in the spirit.
I'm here, Gerald. Nothing can separate us.
Teach them the declarations of the Holy Spirit.
Let your confidence in me rise up.
This movie will go far beyond what you could have ever imagined.
Stay focused on me.
Gerald, I only want you to have my best. Rest in me.
My hand is on this project. it's time to move forward.
I've set things up for you. My favor is on your life.
Trust me, Gerald. Have faith in me as you move forward, knowing that I am with you.
I've blessed you with wisdom. Use it.
There's great profit in spending time praying in the spirit and spending time with me.
You will be an example of my goodness and trusting me.
Many are watching."

Things God spoke to me:

"Be intentional. Intentional to spend time with me.
To read my word.
Be intentional to want to know me more and more.
Be intentional every day. You don't have to be validated.
I'm the only one who needs to validate you.
Trust me that I'm speaking to you and through you.
Yes, in this quiet place I can speak to you.
I want you to trust me and me only. Not the validation
of men.
Gerald, build this place of prayer. I'm here, son.
Gerald, I know how much you desire to follow the
Holy Spirit.
Trust as you have been spending time with
me that I'm leading you to the right place.
Trust me."

Chapter Seventeen

PURPOSE

It always amazes me that God sometimes calls us to a place that seems unfamiliar. This is similar to the story of Abram when he was told, "Go from your country, your people, and your father's household to the land I will show you" (Genesis 12:1). As I was called to what seemed like an unfamiliar place, which was Oakland Church, I first had to trust that I had heard from God. That requires knowing His voice. *How do you get to know God's voice?* By spending time with Him.

After being married to Karen for 28 years, I know her voice. I could be in a crowd of people calling my name, and if Karen were in that group, I could single her voice out from all the rest. That's because I spend intimate time with her, talking with her all the time. In the same way, we learn to discern the voice of our Heavenly Father. Many voices may try to capture our attention, but we must know when it is God speaking to us. John 10:27-28 says, "My sheep hear my voice, and I know them, and they follow me: And I give unto them eternal life; and they shall never perish, neither shall any man pluck them out of my hand."

So, there I was at Oakland Church for my first meeting. It was a Wednesday night at a men's fellowship, and on this particular night, out of about 60 men in the meeting, I was the only Black man in the room. It kind of felt like the first day of school, not knowing anybody. It was a little awkward, to say the least. As Pastor Dominic began to speak that night, he talked about a little book called *Who You Are in Christ*. He mentioned that, many years ago, he would read the declarations from this booklet out loud and record them on a tape recorder. When he said that, I thought to myself, *"I could do that!"* After all, recording my voice is what I do for a living.

As soon as I got home, I took that little booklet that had been passed out to all the men, and I began reading and recording one of the declarations. I then added music to it. As a voice-over talent, I read it in a dramatic way with the right inflection and found the perfect melodic music to enhance the message in the recorded declarations. After I recorded it and listened back with the music, I thought, *I might be on to something*. I sent it to my wife, who loved it. Then Karen sent it to her friend LaDonna, who sent it to her husband, Marcus.

Marcus called me and said, "Man, this is great! We need to send this to Pastor D!"

Next Wednesday night at the men's meeting, Pastor Dominic walked up to me and said, "Gerald, I loved those declarations you recorded. Do you think you would be interested in leading the men in some declarations on Wednesday nights?"

Honestly, when he said that, my heart sank! I thought, "Me? Lead the men in spiritual declarations?"

Now, I had served as the emcee for lots of concerts before, standing in front of thousands of people and introducing artists like Aretha Franklin, The Temptations, The Isley Brothers, and Chaka Khan. The list goes on and on from my radio career. But I never thought I would have the opportunity to lead something from a church pulpit (technically, the basement of the church, but still). Finally, after all the things I had done for the world, I was getting a chance to truly use my voice for the Lord. I knew I had no other choice but to accept the offer.

Every Wednesday, I led the men in declarations. This was confirmation that the move to this church was the right thing to do—I was finally off the bench and in the game. Here is an example of one of the declarations:

Declarations of the Secret Place

Father, I will dwell in the secret place of refuge.
In this secret place is where I will find rest.
You are my place of safety, and I trust You.
You rescue me from every trap, from every deadly disease.
In this secret place, Your faithful promises are my armor and protection.
I am not afraid of the terrors at night or the disasters that strike at midday.
I am safe with You in this secret place.
A thousand may fall at my side, ten thousand at my right hand.
But these evils shall not come near me or my family.
Because, Lord, I dwell in Your secret place.
I stand strong with this armor of protection.
Lord, You are my refuge. You are the Most High. My shelter.
No evil will conquer me. No plague will come near my home.
Angels are protecting me and my family wherever we go.
Thank You, Father. Because of my love for You, You will rescue me.
You protect me because I trust in Your name.
When I call on You, You answer.
Thank You, Lord, that You are with me in trouble.
That You will rescue me and honor me.
Lord, thank You for a long life—a long life of Your salvation.

Every Wednesday at Oakland Church, I stood before 50 to 60 men and led them in spiritual affirmations. I realized I could not depend on my experience or skills for this great task. So, each week, I would ask the Lord,

"What do You want me to say to the men this week?" And each time, I would be led to something that aligned with the speaker's message. That is how the Holy Spirit works, by delivering a message to those who need to hear a specific word. I took this opportunity to minister to the men very seriously. I never wanted to show up unprepared. Spending time with God and finding out what He wanted me to say was crucial to the process.

Not only did I do the declarations live in front of the men every Wednesday night, but I also pre-recorded them in the studio, added music, and sent MP3 files to all the men so they could listen on their own time and share them with others. What I continued to learn, and what I hoped the men also learned, was the power of our words. Proverbs 18:21 says, "Death and life are in the power of the tongue: and they that love it shall eat the fruit thereof." Even though I always knew this, I had to ask myself, "Why am I not paying attention to what I am saying? Why do we let things come out of our mouths that are not true about us?" As I led the men in these powerful declarations, I was also finally learning who God had called me to be. Now, it was time for me to walk in it.

Recently, I created a YouTube channel www.youtube.com/@geraldmcbride8595 that has all of these declarations, from walking in love, forgiveness, who we are in Christ, patience, healing, and more. It's funny that because of my rich, deep voice, I've sometimes been labeled as "the Voice of God." But leading people in His word and helping them understand who they are in Christ is the real meaning of being the voice of God.

* * *

During this time, our daughter Alana's career had truly blossomed. As I mentioned earlier, she had graduated from Howard University with a degree in chemical engineering. We were so excited about this amazing accomplishment, but when she graduated, Alana decided to go in a completely different direction.

She had always wanted to be a makeup artist. After graduation, she took a job at various malls, working for makeup companies like MAC, doing makeup for customers at the counter. At first, this didn't make much sense to us. After all the hard work of earning a chemical engineering degree, five years of dedication, why would you go work for very little money in a mall doing makeup?

But Alana had vision. After several years of building her skills and reputation, she began gaining personal clients. What started as a mall job grew into a major career as a freelance makeup artist, working with top-name clients such as Project Runway, Nike, Burberry, Harper's Bazaar, Lauryn Hill, and many others. Yes, Alana became a successful makeup entrepreneur.

Karen believes that one reason Alana thought this goal was attainable is that she saw me pursuing my own entrepreneurial path. That may be true, but what I've always seen in her is persistence, sacrifice, and the determination to become who she's meant to be. As I've always taught all our kids: don't just find a job — find your passion. What is your gift? What would you do for free because you love it so much? When you discover your gift and follow your passion, the money will follow.

In the summer of 2021, Alana and her longtime boyfriend, Daniel, who had been living together in California, finally decided to get married. Karen and I were thrilled with the news. We had been praying they would make this decision. They planned a wonderful wedding for late August.

A couple of months before the wedding, Alana called with an unusual request: could I pick up her dad, Bobby, and take him shopping for a suit? This may seem strange, being asked to take your wife's ex-husband shopping, but when faced with situations like this, I always ask myself, "What would God want me to do?" Without hesitation, I agreed.

Bobby had hit on some hard times, losing both of his parents and being unemployed for some time. He needed help, not having any transportation and living on a limited Social Security budget. One

Saturday morning, I picked up Bobby from the rental house that he was leasing from his frat brother in Pontiac. When I pulled up in the driveway, he immediately came out as if he was excited to get out of the house for a while. Mind you, this was the first time Bobby and I had ever spent any one-on-one time together, so this felt like a small opportunity to get to know each other a little more.

When he got into my Mercedes SUV, he seemed very impressed with the car.

"What kind of Mercedes is this? This is nice!"

"It's a Mercedes GLE Coupe," I replied.

I'm not sure I noticed what he saw, but he then said, "Look at all the white people looking at us in this car!" I could only laugh at his comment. Bobby was never one to be lost for words, and during the ride, he pretty much controlled the conversation while I just listened.

Bobby was a well-educated person, very articulate in his old-school ways and very opinionated about political issues, mainly because he spent most of his time alone in the house, where his only form of entertainment was the TV. He was filled with all kinds of political facts that he picked up from CNN and Fox News. As we rode in the car to the suit store, he shared so many political views that you would have thought he worked for a news channel.

We arrived at Baron's Men's Wear and began looking for a suit. Of course, Alana had chosen a color to coordinate with the wedding party: a steel-blue-gray suit, which I would wear as well. I helped him pick out a suit and tie, then took him to the tailor in the same building. Afterwards, I took him to his favorite fried fish place to grab carryout and dropped him off at home. This would be the last time we saw each other until the wedding.

Two months later, the wedding took place in beautiful Big Sur, California. I have never seen a place with such stunning ocean views. This was my first time in that part of California, and it looked just like what I had seen on postcards and on TV: huge waves crashing onto the mountainside rocks along a narrow highway. It was so breathtaking that Karen said, "Gerald, slow down!" With my love for just riding in the car and looking at scenery—something I do at home all the time—this was the ultimate opportunity to drive and see breathtaking views. I could have driven for hours, surprised by each and every turn around the twisting highway.

The house where the wedding was taking place was just as beautiful: a tri-level dream house with walls of windows and decks that surrounded the entire structure with ocean views. As I stepped out onto the deck, I noticed the house sat on a hillside with gardens of beautiful flowers, offering even more views of the ocean and mountains, all accompanied by the sound of crashing waves.

In Big Sur, California, the fog drapes the rugged coastline like a silvery veil, softening the jagged edges of the Santa Lucia Mountains as they plunge into the Pacific Ocean. It rolls in from the sea thick and heavy, like a vast white ocean flowing over the canyons and forests, leaving only the tallest peaks and trees jutting out like islands. The fog muffles sound and light, casting the world into a quiet, ethereal place. At sunrise or sunset, the mist glows with faint golds and pinks, lending the landscape a dreamlike, almost surreal quality. It was so beautiful!

As I stepped out of the house that morning, fog covered the land, offering just a glimpse of the ocean and the mountains. As I stared out, I thought, "What a paradise!" The people who live here are so blessed to call such a beautiful place home. That morning, as I searched for a place to have my quiet time with the Lord, this scenery provided the perfect setting. I remember sitting there, watching hummingbirds hover right before my eyes. This is where God would speak to me about something very important.

As I was gathered there with all of my family, God made it clear that this was one of the reasons for marrying Karen: to provide a family for her and Alana. With Karen, Alana, and Bobby all being only children, there was practically no support on either side of the family. But because of our marriage, this would provide Alana with a brother, a sister, a brother-in-law, a niece, and a nephew who were all there for one of the most important days of her life. Is this part of the reason God spoke to me in that audible voice I mentioned earlier? I believe it was, given the importance of this day when we all came together, signifying this blended family. As I looked around with all of us there, I wondered what it would have looked like without us, since we were the only family there to represent Alana.

As the wedding proceeded, Bobby and I escorted Alana down the aisle together to join her new husband, Daniel. It was a beautiful, historic family moment I'll never forget. In that moment, it seemed as though God was truly pleased with this act of obedience that would be a great blessing to others. In Hebrews 13:16, it says: "Do not forget to do good and to share with others, for with such sacrifices God is pleased." It's not the size of the sacrifice, but the heart behind it—when done freely, not for recognition, but out of compassion and love—that carries deep spiritual weight.

* * *

In 2022, I began to see myself differently. I spoke with more boldness and expressed myself more in my writing. By this time, my writing skills had improved, and my desire to write grew stronger. I was learning to be confident in what God was calling me to do. At the beginning of the year, during a service, Pastor Dom spoke about this being a year to move on your dreams. When I heard that, something registered within me. I had been sitting on this dream long enough—it was time to move! I knew in my spirit it was time to make this movie happen. All this time, I had been trying to sell the idea to someone in Hollywood, but now I believed that God was telling me to do it myself. *But how could I come up with the $2.5 million that Hollywood proposed for making the movie? Where would I start?* These questions ran through my mind as I tried to figure out the process of making a film.

I remembered a message from Joyce Meyer: "If you plan to step out on faith, then you have to begin to take some steps. Don't be afraid. If you begin to head in the wrong direction, God knows how to get you back on track." Psalm 37:23-24 says, "The steps of a good man are ordered by the LORD..." So, I began to take steps.

The first big step I took toward actualizing my dream was reaching out to Ashlee Woolridge, whom I had met at a film workshop hosted by Transformation Films Institute several years back. She had previously told me that if I were ever interested in making the film myself, she would be more than happy to help.

Things God spoke to me:

"Stay close to me, Gerald.
This is where you'll find my peace.
The peace that the world can't give.
I'm here, Gerald. Pay attention to what I'm saying to you.
Continue to follow me.
Yes, I've given you a job to do, and you have done it well.
I need you right where I have you, Gerald.
Yes, there will be an anointing of my spirit on your movie.
People will like watching and won't know why.
Trust me that I'm ordering your steps.
Decree and declare over your movie that God's hand is on this film.
There's anointing on it. People will watch it over and over again.
Gerald, receive my protection. Know that my hand is on your life.
The great harvest is coming! You don't have to know how.
Just know it's coming. I will take care of you and your family.
Stay close to me as I give you instructions.
As you move, I move."

Chapter EIGHTEEN

BLACK ICE

In January 2022, I began pre-production of *Black Ice*. Alongside Ashlee Woolridge, we scheduled our shoot to begin on May 15, 2022, but there was a lot to be done before then. We first created a budget. We figured out a way to make this a locally produced film for under 150 thousand, which meant we would have to wear multiple hats to make it work. We cut every corner possible with our budget, but at the same time, we made sure everyone who wanted to be involved got paid something. It might not be top dollar, but if they wanted to lend a hand, they would get paid something. The next step was auditioning actors, starting with the lead.

I had seen how well Arthur Cartwright performed in the pitch trailer, so I reached out to him to see if he would be interested in playing the lead for the full-length film. He was thrilled to be a part of it. Ashlee and I continued breaking down the script, determining which scenes to shoot on which days, how many crew members we would need, and the cost for each day. In the meantime, I contacted a talent agency, Production

Plus, to send over actors for certain roles. Finding the right actors seemed easy; each character took only two auditions before I found the best fit.

Jaclene Wilks was one of the women who auditioned for the role of Olivia. In the movie, Olivia is one of the main characters, the supervisor of the Butzel Recreation Center in Detroit's urban area. She runs the day-to-day operations and hires Robert Buck Taylor, who has to work there after his release from prison to complete his community service. Originally, the character's name was Karen, but due to the controversy surrounding that name, I decided to change it. Jaclene, with her warm personality and radiant smile, was a perfect fit. She nailed the audition. After hearing her do a table read with Arthur, it truly felt like the perfect match.

Next was casting the role of Corey. Corey was the street teenager who worked in the streets selling drugs for his thug drug dealer, uncle Ray, who tried to keep Corey from playing hockey, claiming, "He didn't have time to play hockey because he needed Corey in the streets making money for the family business." I needed someone with a tough Detroit look who could bring natural grit to the role without seeming forced. I found a young man named Davante Adams, who did an amazing job during the audition and took it to another level once we got on set. During rehearsals and auditions, he assured me that he could cry on the spot if needed. I told him, "Hold the tears till I really need them."

Finding young Black actors who could play hockey was going to be nearly impossible, especially locally. I reached out to an organization called Detroit Ice Dreams, which played at Jack Adams Ice Rink, the same location where we planned to shoot most of the film. I contacted the director, Cynthia Warsaw, to ask whether she had any players with outgoing personalities who might be interested in acting. She sent Ashlee and me several pictures, and after auditions, we cast Tyler Moore as JoJo, the goalie who lacked confidence and interest in playing hockey. Javonn Crittendon was cast as his teammate Mike, who spends most of his time searching for and wanting a relationship with his father, whom he never knew. Then there was King Moore as Flash, the teammate who gets his 16-year-old girlfriend pregnant, is forced to tell her parents, and steps up to the responsibility of being a father at a young age.

Then came assembling the filming crew. I reached out to Hugh Hatten of Team 3 Productions, who was very helpful. Hugh and I had worked on several projects together, but this would be our first film. I hired him as my director of photography, and he also helped assemble a crew of lighting technicians, grips, assistant camera operators, and production assistants. Even though the project was months away, they all committed to being part of the making of *Black Ice*.

A few weeks into pre-production, a fellow church member approached me after service and said, "Hey, I hear you're making a movie."

"Yes, I am," I replied.

"I have camera equipment you can use, and don't worry about paying me until after the movie makes some money."

"Wow! Thank you so much, Dan!" I was truly grateful for the blessing from fellow church member Dan Cobb.

Dan's camera package included RED cameras, high-end equipment used for major films, along with lenses, tripods, cables, camera focus remotes, and more. It was a complete, professional setup. This was yet another confirmation that God's hand was on this project. It is true that when God gives you a vision, He provides provision. It is also amazing how people are placed in your life at just the right moment to encourage you.

I also reached out to my good friends David and Lyn Talbert, producers of *Jingle Jangle, Baggage Claim, First Sunday, Last Christmas*, and more. The great thing about having friends like them is that they never sugarcoat anything. They tell you the truth. They had seen my passion for years and did whatever they could to support me. When I told them I was going to produce, finance, and direct this movie myself, I'll never forget Lyn's words: "Go for it, Gerald." I'm not sure if she understood the impact of those words at the time, but in that moment,

I felt an extra boost of confidence. It was like Popeye getting his spinach. A few encouraging words can make all the difference in a person's life. The Bible says, "Life and death are in the power of the tongue." We must remember to speak life into people's dreams. It could be as simple as saying, "Go for it."

Everything seemed to be falling into place, except for the money. I had the actors, the film crew, the equipment, and the production schedule, but no funding. This was truly stepping out on faith, believing that God would provide. Every single day in my prayer time, I sought the Lord's guidance because there were so many decisions to make. Karen and I initially thought we would raise money through investors, offering a 5% return. We received one response from someone willing to invest $5,000, but that was a long way from the $150,000 we needed. We also didn't have peace about borrowing money without knowing if we could pay it back. This was my first film, and I was still unsure how it would all turn out. Yes, I was stepping into unfamiliar territory, but I knew this was where God wanted me. Still, borrowing money from individuals wasn't the path He intended for me, so we continued praying for direction.

By April 2022, our shoot date was less than 30 days away. The actors were learning their lines, weekly rehearsals and table reads were happening, and crew meetings were in full swing. One challenge we needed to solve was securing an affordable hockey rink for 30 days. Many rinks in Metro Detroit were either unavailable or extremely expensive, costing between $150 to $200 per hour. That meant we were looking at over $100,000 just for rink rental alone, an amount that could crush our budget.

Finding a rink available for 30 straight days was another hurdle. Finally, I got a contact for Jack Adams Butzel Rink, the location we had always wanted since the story was based on the Butzel Rec Center. The rink was owned by the City of Detroit, which meant navigating government bureaucracy to find the person in charge. After days of effort, I finally got Ricardo Marble on the phone.

"Hello?"

"Is this Ricardo Marble?"

"Speaking."

"This is Gerald McBride."

Before I could explain, he said, "Gerald McBride! Man, let me tell you something. I know your daughter and son-in-law, Brandy and Dway Mitchell."

"Oh yeah?" I replied. "How do you know them?"

"I used to go to their church, Via Dolorosa." Then he added, "Let me tell you another story. About 20 years ago, I was going to Spec Howard School of Broadcasting. Your office was on the second floor. I knocked on your door, I told you I was interested in doing voice-overs, and you invited me in, showed me your studio, and gave me great advice. I never forgot that day!"

I was touched by his words. "Wow," was all I could say.

Then Ricardo asked, "What can I do for you?"

"Well, I'm shooting a movie called *Black Ice* about young Black kids learning to play hockey in Detroit. I need to use the rink for 30 days in May."

"No problem," he said. "Whatever you need, Gerald, you got it. The hockey season ends on May 7th; after that, the rink is all yours."

Then came the big question: "How much is it?"

He answered, "It won't cost you anything."

Wow! It was almost as if I had seen a miracle happen before my eyes. Once again, God provided. The lesson learned is, always treat everyone with respect, be willing to help if you can, because you never know how your paths may cross again.

With just days left before shooting, everything was in place, except for the money. My budget had now increased to be able pay everyone. And just like that, five days before our scheduled start on May 23rd, I received an email from the SBA. My company had qualified for a $180,000 loan, and by faith, I decided to take it. I would later find out that it would fall short of what I needed to complete the film. But God is always faithful. He would never bring me this far and not provide.

Things God spoke to me:

"As you have told others, write down what I am speaking to you.
Prepare yourself to receive the blessing I have for you.
It will be greater than you ever imagined.
Keep me first. Trust me first.
Always remember I will never leave you or forsake you.
I am always here to guide and protect you from the enemy.
Read John 10-10. I have an abundant life for you.
Nothing missing.
This blessing will flow to your children
and children's children from generation to generation.
They will experience the blessing that is on your life.
As I did it for Abraham, I will do it for you.
It is an everlasting covenant.
I want to show the world what a commitment to me means.
They need to see this so that they desire to come close to me.
This is me speaking to you, Gerald.
The world is full of greed and insecurity.
They need to see good examples of my love.
Yes, I have placed people in your life for a reason
to get you in the place where I have called you to be.

Follow me. I will guide you."
"Gerald, this is where I can speak to you.
There are so many distractions.
But this quiet time with me is where I can speak to you and direct you.
Trust me. As you pray in the spirit, I can give you more revelation.
Be bold to tell people what I have told you.
Don't be afraid or ashamed to share what I've told you.
Let it be a blessing to others.
Be confident in what I have spoken to you.

Chapter Nineteen

A Life of Meaning

As I continued to step out in faith, I began to witness events unfold that confirmed I was on the right path. There is nothing more gratifying than knowing you are walking in the perfect will of God.

We began shooting on May 23rd at Butzel Recreation Center in the heart of Detroit. The shoot started early in the morning, with the crew loading in equipment and reviewing the day's scene schedule. The high-quality RED cameras and all their accessories, which had been loaned to me, were carefully unpacked and assembled. The crew was amazed at the level of professional equipment we had access to, and their excitement was contagious.

As we began shooting, I was surprised at how comfortable I felt directing, despite it being my first time in the role. It became clear that my past experiences in directing voice-over actors, producing commercial spots, and coaching talent over the years had all prepared me for this moment. It's incredible how God has a plan and wastes nothing. Even the smallest tasks, those we might see as unimportant, can be the very tools He uses to prepare us for our future. One directing technique I found effective was allowing the actors some freedom in delivering their lines. I would tell them, "Here's what I wrote, but if you have a better way of saying it, let me hear it." If I liked their version, I recorded both takes. In hindsight, this approach gave me valuable options in the editing process, options I was grateful to have later.

Each day on set, my confidence grew, and I continued learning so much along the way. One major challenge I encountered was underestimating how long it would take to set up each scene. While I initially planned to shoot three to four scenes per day, the reality was that the lighting setup often took longer than expected. Every location, especially inside the hockey rink, required different lighting configurations, which significantly slowed us down. As a result, on some days we could shoot only one or two scenes, which pushed our schedule behind. I quickly realized that the 30 days we had initially planned for shooting would not be enough, and that we would surpass our budget.

After the initial 30-day shoot, we had about 70% of the film completed. By that time, I had already spent the $150,000 I had budgeted, and I knew the remaining $30,000 of the $180,000 I had received wouldn't be enough. Taking a break from shooting allowed me to review the footage, identify gaps, and create a revised plan to complete the film.

Also, during the hiatus, I would get more ideas for the movie and would add some additional scenes. This experience was an invaluable lesson in time management and budgeting, which ended up being a $300,000 crash course in filmmaking.

Meanwhile, just weeks before filming would resume, Karen enrolled us in the School of Ministry at Oakland Church. Classes were every Tuesday night from 6:30 to 9:00, and no matter what was happening with the film, I made it a priority to attend. Who would have thought

I'd be in ministry school? With each class, my understanding of God deepened as I understood His character, His actions, His love, and His expectations for us. The instructors, wise and experienced biblical scholars, shared their insights, and I found myself eagerly anticipating each lesson. Through this two-year course, I developed a more intimate relationship with God, realizing that getting to know Him is a lifelong journey. Will we ever have all of the answers? Probably not.

We were given several books to read each semester. One book that stood out to me during the program was *Driven by Eternity* by John Bevere. To this day, I continue to revisit it. This book reinforced the reality that our time on earth is short and that what truly matters is how we prepare for eternity. Our daily choices, how we use our gifts, and what we accomplish for God's Kingdom all shape our destiny beyond this life. Now, being in my sixties, I reflect more on what comes after this life. With more years behind me than ahead, I understand the urgency of making every day count.

Through the School of Ministry, as the different instructors explained to us, many of us would find our calling, purpose, or ministry in life. I discovered that my deeper purpose was in writing. I was never particularly skilled in English or creative writing during my school years, but now God was placing this ability within me. Had it always been there, lying dormant? Perhaps. Or maybe I had been so focused on making money that I overlooked my true calling. Either way, I now felt a renewed sense of purpose and who I really was. As you spend time with God, He will reveal these things to you. Several people in the Bible experienced pivotal moments when they realized they were made for a greater purpose, a better life in line with God's calling. Here are some of the most compelling examples:

1. **Joseph (Genesis 37–50)** Revelation: Through dreams and suffering. Journey: Sold into slavery by his brothers, falsely accused, and imprisoned. Realization: Despite hardship, Joseph eventually became the second most powerful man in Egypt. He

recognized that God used his suffering for a higher purpose—to save many people during a famine. Key Verse: "You intended to harm me, but God intended it for good to accomplish what is now being done, the saving of many lives." (Genesis 50:20)

2. **Moses (Exodus 3–4)** Revelation: A burning bush and a direct call from God. Journey: Raised in Pharaoh's palace, fled to the wilderness after killing an Egyptian, then called by God to deliver Israel. Realization: Moses initially resisted, thinking he wasn't worthy or eloquent. But he came to embrace his identity as God's chosen leader. Key Verse: "Now go; I will help you speak and will teach you what to say." (Exodus 4:12)

3. **Esther (Esther 4)** Revelation: Through Mordecai's challenge. Journey: A Jewish girl who became queen of Persia. Realization: She risked her life to save her people, recognizing her royal position had a divine purpose. Key Verse: "And who knows but that you have come to your royal position for such a time as this?" (Esther 4:14)

4. **David (1 Samuel 16–17)** Revelation: Through being anointed and defeating Goliath. Journey: Young shepherd, overlooked by his family, yet chosen by God. Realization: David understood that his strength came from God, and he was destined to be a leader. Key Verse: "The Lord who rescued me from the paw of the lion and the paw of the bear will rescue me from the hand of this Philistine." (1 Samuel 17:37)

5. **Paul (Acts 9)** Revelation: A blinding encounter with Jesus. Journey: Persecutor of Christians turned apostle. Realization: Paul's radical transformation revealed his new purpose: to spread the Gospel to the Gentiles. Key Verse: "This man is my chosen instrument to proclaim my name to the Gentiles..." (Acts 9:15)

6. **Ruth (Ruth 1–4)** Revelation: Through loyalty and obedience. Journey: A Moabite widow who chose to follow her mother-in-law's God. Realization: Her faithfulness led her to become part of the lineage of King David—and eventually Jesus. Key Verse: "Your people will be my people and your God my God." (Ruth 1:16)

Looking back, my career in voice-over production, creating radio spots for legends like Chris Tucker, Janet Jackson, Earth, Wind & Fire, Jamie Foxx, Katt Williams, Gladys Knight, Prince, and Luther Vandross, was fulfilling, but I now see it in a different light. Yes, making a living is necessary, but discovering and walking in our true purpose is even greater. Not everyone is called to the pulpit, but we all have a role in building God's kingdom with the gifts that God has deposited in us. Your purpose could be that you will become wealthy in your field and use the money to finance the Kingdom by giving generously to your church and to people. It may also be to serve in other areas where your talents are needed: children's ministry, kitchen, maintenance, ushering, TV ministry, parking lot, and so much more. All of these things are important in supporting and building the body of Christ.

One afternoon, after leaving church on my way home, the Lord began speaking to me about calling my ex-wife, Deanne. To be honest, I thought, "Is this you, Lord? Really call Deanne?" We had a pretty good relationship, so calling her wouldn't be out of the ordinary, but what the Lord wanted me to tell her seemed a little uncomfortable. I knew that Deanne had been dealing with some health issues.

Our church was having an evening healing service with a guest evangelist from South Africa known for his miraculous healing services, and the Lord wanted me to invite her. When it came to receiving messages about another person's well-being, I knew it was God. I couldn't just ignore what I was prompted to do, so I finally called her.

"Hello?"

"Hey, Deanne, it's Gerald."

"Hey! What's up?"

"Well, I was calling to invite you to our healing service. I know you've been having problems walking, and you're not supposed to be like this! God wants you healed! Now listen, Karen and I can come pick you up if we have to."

All of a sudden, there was just silence on the phone. Then I heard her whimpering.

"Deanne, it's going to be okay. God loves you so much." Then there was silence as she continued to cry.

"I'll call you back," Deanne said.

A few minutes later, my son called me.

"Hey, Mom just called me and said you invited her to church."

"That's right. We're having a healing service tonight at 6:30."

Jaz responded, "I'll bring her."

That night during praise and worship, Karen and I were sitting in the front row of the church. I kept glancing back to see if Deanne had arrived. Finally, Jaz walked in with his mother and seated her about halfway back. I whispered to Karen, "I think I should go get her and bring her up front with us." Karen agreed.

So I went back and told Deanne that she needed to come up front and sit with us. At first, she seemed unsure and hesitant, but finally agreed. I helped her with her walker, and we slowly made our way up front, seating her next to Karen and me.

The evangelist preached an amazing sermon on the power of healing and then had us pray for the person next to us. Karen and I immediately began to lay hands on Deanne, pleading the blood of Jesus and decreeing God's promises over her body. As we did this, Deanne began to cry. It was an emotional moment and the first time ever that I had the opportunity to pray for my ex-wife.

This was truly a rare moment of God's power and His love. What had happened to us in our past was irrelevant. My only hope was that she would receive her healing.

***

In the summer of 2023, I resumed filming, working around my schedule and the availability of the crew and actors. By this time, I had lost most of my support producers, who had moved on to other projects, so I had to take on multiple roles, handling wardrobe, transportation, craft services, props, and practically anything else that needed to be done. Despite the challenges, this break gave me a valuable opportunity to refine the script.

During ministry school, God revealed new ideas to me, prompting me to rewrite and reshoot certain scenes. One pivotal moment came when a speaker in class discussed the significance of the cross and our identity in Christ. That day, God gave me the idea to incorporate Mark 5:36 into the film: "Don't be afraid; just believe." This became the movie's central theme. I also wanted to highlight the true meaning of the cross, beyond it being a piece of jewelry. Without the movie being too churchy, it makes the point that the cross isn't just a piece of jewelry around someone's neck or a good-luck charm hanging from a rearview mirror. Hopefully, after seeing this film, they will look at it differently to better understand its real meaning.

In one scene, the main character, Robert Buck Taylor, is released from jail and returns home to his grandmother, a devout believer.

She hands him a cross and says, "I think you should start wearing this again."

Buck dismisses it, saying, "For what, Grandma? For good luck?"

She gently responds, "No, it's a symbol that represents Him. Jesus died so you could have a better life. It is in the Word. Don't be afraid, just believe."

I truly believe God allowed me to pause production so I could receive these revelations in ministry school, which ultimately enriched the film. With God, nothing is ever wasted. Even our perceived setbacks and mistakes can be used for a greater purpose.

Things God spoke to me:

"Gerald, I know the desires of your heart.
Trust me. I shall lead you.
I put these dreams and desires in you.
I'm here, Gerald.
The enemy can't get in here where you are next to me.
My favor surrounds you.
Trust the things I've said to you in prayer.
I'm here. Know how special you are to me.
I'm using you now for my glory.
Glorify me when you do these things which I have called you to do."

Chapter Twenty

It's a Wrap!

Graduating from the School of Ministry and finishing the editing of the movie were two great events of my life that happened simultaneously. Karen graduated with honors, and I just graduated. I realized that I should have turned in more of my homework assignments. Regardless, finishing ministry school was a massive achievement in my life. But more importantly, I discovered the purpose God had for my life: a ministry on the screen. If I could create films that inspire people, leaving the theater or watching at home with something to think about, then I would know I had done what God called me to do.

My movie *Black Ice: The Rhythm* was released in Emagine Theaters on May 31, 2024, for a two-week run, selling out multiple shows and receiving tremendous reviews. As Karen and I watched the audience react with laughter, tears, and heartfelt testimonies, we were grateful and humbled to know that all the hard work and sacrifice had been worth it. We could now look forward to the opportunity to create more films.

My thought after this two-week run in local theaters, with an overwhelming response, was that I could extend our run by adding more cities. But because of other blockbuster films like *Bad Boys 4: Ride or Die* and *Twister*, there was no room left for my independent film. Even though it did extremely well, those movies took precedence over what was showing in the theaters at the time, which pushed my movie out. At that point, I could never get the film buyers who are responsible for getting films in theaters to buy into giving me another chance at a theater run. So, after the successful buzz with *Black Ice: The Rhythm*, I was sidelined.

To be quite honest, I was a little disappointed and frustrated. The film buyers wouldn't even return my calls. At this point, I realized that trying to get into the theaters and staying there for a while as an independent film was a lot more difficult than I had anticipated. The only thing I could do now was try and get a streaming deal.

On the heels of my theater run came another faith-based movie called *The Forge*. With its August 2024 release, it did amazing business in theaters. After watching it, I felt audiences would get the same kind of emotional, feel-good inspiration from my film. *The Forge* was written and inspired by a sermon about a group of young men who come together to disciple another, helping him build a relationship with Christ and turn his life around. My film wasn't quite as scriptural, but still told the story of a young African American man who loved hockey.

In a gritty semi-pro hockey showdown, teenage player Robert engages in a relentless on-ice brawl against a rival white player, with no referees to stop them. The fight intensifies, culminating in Robert delivering a devastating blow to the opponent's head, leading to a shocking five-year prison sentence for attempted murder, with all hope seeming to be extinguished.

Fresh out of a three-year prison stint, Robert faces an unexpected challenge: forming a hockey team in an all-black urban neighborhood with a neglected ice rink. Under the watchful eye of his supervisor,

Olivia, he must transform roller-skating prodigies from a nearby rink into ice hockey stars. But in doing so, he faces many obstacles in his own life while also teaching the team of young boys the same principles he's learning to overcome with the power of faith, perseverance, and forgiveness.

In this process of waiting again, now for a distribution deal, it was all about God's timing. I had waited all this time to finally get the movie made, and now I was faced with the challenge and process of waiting some more. It was about finding the right distribution company for the film. A distribution company deal is crucial for a new independent film because it directly affects whether the film reaches an audience and generates revenue.

Here's why it's so important:

1. **Access to Audiences** • Distributors have established networks with theaters, streaming platforms (e.g., Netflix, Hulu), TV broadcasters, and international markets. • Without a distributor, it's extremely hard for an indie film to break into these channels.

2. **Marketing and Promotion** • Distributors often handle or support marketing efforts, creating trailers, posters, press kits, and coordinating festival entries and PR. • For indie filmmakers with limited budgets, this professional support is essential to generate buzz and awareness.

3. **Sales and Revenue** • A distribution deal enables monetization: theatrical releases, digital rentals/sales, VOD/DVD/Blu-ray, and international sales. • Distributors negotiate licensing deals and ensure proper tracking and collection of revenue.

4. **Legitimacy and Visibility** • A distribution company's involvement often lends credibility, making it easier to attract press coverage, reviews, and festival placements. • It signals to the industry that your film is commercially viable.

5. **Legal and Logistical Support** • Distribution companies handle complex rights management, legal clearances, delivery specs, and technical requirements for different platforms and territories.

6. **Long-Term Strategy** • Good distributors think beyond just the release—they strategize how to build the film's lifespan across multiple markets and windows.

In short, a distribution deal turns a completed film into a commercial product with real audience reach and income potential. For most independent filmmakers, it's the bridge between art and sustainability.

I began looking locally for distributors who were primarily responsible for getting many films onto platforms like Tubi. While some films have had success on this platform, I felt this movie had greater mass appeal and the potential to reach a larger audience. My wife's boss at Music Hall caught wind of my film and suggested to her that I reach out to his longtime friend Mark Holdom, who was an aggregator. A film aggregator is a company or a person who acts as the middleman between the filmmaker and the distribution company. After a couple of conversations with Mark, he began seeking out distribution companies that might be interested in the film.

While he was looking, I was also putting out feelers in other relationships I had established in the industry. To be quite honest, people weren't jumping at the opportunity to offer me a deal, but after getting such rave reviews from my short theater run, it was confirmation that I had something special. It seemed as though everywhere I looked, there was a middleman who promised to introduce me to a deal, but a lot of them were unsuccessful in the attempt.

I had to realize that God had a plan. It seemed like a maze. As I ran into one wall, I was forced to try a different way. As this door was shut, I would try another door and another and so on. I was truly continuing to live out what I had written about in the movie: "Faith and perseverance."

Weeks would go by, but still no deal. Mark would mention from time to time that he had a couple of companies that seemed interested, but for some reason, I didn't think that was the way to go. I began circling back to a contact I had made with a guy named Larry Frenzel. Larry was one of the producers of the film that I mentioned earlier, *The Forge* by the Kendrick brothers. It was now the fall of 2024, and *The Forge* was up to about $42 million in box office sales! My thought was that since this film did so well and my film was along the same genre, it would be great if I could get a pitch to Sony to take on this film.

After weeks of convincing Larry to get me a pitch before Sony to take on this project, we finally got our chance to get in front of one of the premier companies in the industry. I knew this was it! If Sony could come up with a substantial marketing budget and take this movie to theaters like they did with the last few films made by the Kendrick brothers, like *The Forge, War Room, Fireproof,* and more, this film could certainly do the same amount of box-office numbers! My thoughts were about what I believed could finally happen for a major financial breakthrough! Yes! This was it!

Then the news came from Larry: "Gerald, unfortunately, Sony decided to pass." My response was, of course, "Why? This film was paid for. It was ready to go. The only thing Sony needed to do was market it. How could they have turned it down? Couldn't they see that this fit had the same emotional and inspirational message and feel as the other films? This was a no-brainer for Sony." Larry explained that there was no explanation for why they said no. It was just "No, we are going to pass on this one."

In prayer time, I struggled for a moment with this letdown. Why didn't God open this door for this big blessing? This could have set me up for life. You immediately start to think, "What did I do wrong?" I felt like I needed some sort of spiritual explanation of why. We are always asking ourselves why things didn't go the way we planned. Why did things we prayed and fasted about, claimed, spoke, and declared over, and made a part of our vision boards tied in with scripture, and so on, not happen? Why?

The only answer I got from the Lord was to trust Him. Don't focus on the money or the fame, but just trust Him. During this time, I would often meditate on Matthew 6:33, which says: "Seek first the kingdom of God and His righteousness, and all these things will be added to you." This verse emphasizes the importance of prioritizing God's will and seeking a relationship with Him above all else, including worldly concerns. It suggests that when believers focus on spiritual priorities, God will provide for their needs. It was a strong message to me to take my eyes off the money and focus on Him.

This is a faith-based message of hope and redemption, which was given to me by the Lord in much prayer. It is my job to deliver the message on the screen and not do it for the money. If I take care of what God has called me to do by being a servant and faithful to what He called me to do, then the money will follow, but I had to learn to keep Him first. You see, I had already started spending the money I anticipated before I even made it. I had made plans for a new house, a car, vacations, and more, assuming the deal would be successful. It was all a part of my vision board. I think all of those things are fine, but we can't let those be our main focus. Remember, "Seek ye first His kingdom." I learned to humble myself before the Lord, and He will direct my paths. God wants you to have all those things, but He doesn't want those things to have you.

December 2024 rolls around, and I decide to circle back to Mark, who has a few companies interested in my film. One in particular was Samuel Goldwyn Films. I was so focused on scoring the big deal with Sony that I didn't realize that Samuel Goldwyn was a pretty big deal! In the middle of December, I made the commitment to sign with them, which proved to be a great deal for the film. Was this the deal I should have been looking at all along? Maybe so.

As January 2025 rolled around, the contract was signed with Samuel Goldwyn Pictures. I would spend weeks working on deliverables: artwork, posters, trailers, interviews, contracts of actors and crew, and more. My suggestion to them was to try to get the film up and running on a platform by February to make the story of these Black hockey players part of Black History Month, but that proved not to be enough time for platforms to accept it and include it in their lineup of films. So, once again, this would require patience and trusting God's timing for the film's release.

The first week of January, I went for my regular checkup at Longevity Clinic. Longevity Clinic is an anti-aging clinic that helps with weight loss, nutrition, gut health, and more. I had been going there for three years. Every six months, they gave me a blood test and told me what kind of shape my body was in and, if needed, what kind of dieting and exercise adjustments I needed to make, and the right vitamins to take. On this particular day, I was there for my checkup and the results of my blood test. The doctor came in and said, "I see something that might be a little alarming. Your white blood cells seem to be a little high."

I have to admit, I'm not the greatest when it comes to understanding medical terms, so I asked, "What does that mean?"

She said with some reluctant hesitation, "It means you could have leukemia."

In a very shocked voice, I said, "Leukemia! You've got to be kidding."

She replied, "It's a slight chance, but I think we should check it out just to make sure."

Of course, I agreed to have it checked out, but in my mind, I thought this had to be a mistake! I've never felt better! I'm healthy, I exercise, I try my best to eat healthy, I'm certainly not overweight, so I'm sure this is just a way over-the-top precautionary diagnosis. So my doctor made the necessary arrangements for me to be seen by a hematologist.

A few days later, I arrived at the hematologist. I do the usual check-in with an African American middle-aged woman at the counter. As soon as she notices my name, she says, "Gerald McBride?" Then she asked, "Are you the Gerald McBride on the radio?"

I replied, "Yes, that's me."

She was thrilled, and word quickly spread through the office about who I was. The other African American nurses looked at me with curiosity, as if they might be my audience.

As I took my seat in the waiting area, I looked around and saw other patients also waiting who looked as though they were dealing with cancer. Some were in wheelchairs, on crutches, walkers, or had someone assisting them. Here I am, healthy, feeling like I'm in the greatest shape of my life, wondering what I'm doing here. I don't belong here. This has got to be a mistake!

As my name is called, I head through the door and into the back. Just like I thought, there are mostly African American nurses talking, as the buzz of me being there was still the conversation. As I walked back to step on the scale and go through the usual steps of the doctor's visit, the nurses came up to talk about my show. One would say, "I heard the battle between Michael Jackson and Prince!" Another would chime in, "Who won that battle?"

I replied, "I can't remember. We have done that battle so many times." Now, a few other ladies gathered around to hear my response. I then ask them, "Who would you vote for in that battle?"

A variety of answers created a debate while they were drawing blood from me. After I was done, one of the nurses asked if we could take a selfie, which I did. This shows how little I cared about the diagnosis and that this seemed like a regular day at the doctor's, where I just happened to run into some of my listeners.

One of the nurses escorted me into the small room to await the doctor. He's the head doctor who runs the hematology office. After about five minutes, he entered the room. He was a tall Caucasian man wearing the typical long white doctor's coat with a few pens in the upper right pocket. He's middle-aged, perhaps a little younger than me, with glasses, and he's a kind of no-nonsense person with a serious look. I didn't feel like he had the bedside manner where I might be able to joke around a little, like I do with my regular doctors. He seemed very straightforward and "let's get down to business."

So it's a quick introduction: "Hi, I'm Dr. ..." "Let's check a few things out." He goes through the regular procedures, looks in my ears, nose, checks my heart and throat. Then he had me lay back on the bed and pressed on my chest, ribs, and abdomen, asking if I feel any discomfort, to which I replied, "No." This was all short and quick. He then takes a seat and looks at the blood report and says, "Your white blood cells are high, which means you have a rare blood cell disease, which means in maybe five years or less you will have leukemia and have to take chemo."

I'm shocked! "What? Are you serious? This has got to be wrong!" I replied. He seemed very calm, as though he was used to hearing people's reactions to a diagnosis like this. So he just sat there with these black-framed glasses on the end of his nose, looking at me. After a moment of realizing what he was saying was real, I gathered my thoughts and said, "So what can I do? Can I exercise more, eat better, or take any medicine to change this?"

He simply replied, "There is nothing you can do."

At that moment, my heart sank in disbelief. I could not believe what I was hearing as I sat there in shock, stunned, and speechless. He then said, "Let's make an appointment a few months from now and see if there is any progress." He then gets up, shakes my hand, and walks out of the room. This was one of the moments in life when you ask God, "What just happened?"

I get myself together and walk out of the room. The office is still buzzing about me being there, and a couple of the ladies are still asking questions about my radio show, but it seemed like I didn't hear them at all, as if I was in a whole other world right trying to figure out what was going on.

As I made my way out, I stopped at the front desk to make my future appointment to see that same doctor again. Once I did that, the girl at the front desk asked if we could also take a selfie, which I did, before heading for the exit. I got in my car and just sat there for a moment, still in disbelief, wondering what I do next. I couldn't help but think, "What about my wife? How would she make it in five years without me?"

For some reason, I began to think about my grandkids and not having the opportunity to see Tandie, who's 14, get married or graduate from college, or Cooper, who would only be 17 years old when I'm gone, and that I wouldn't be around to see him become a young man. You can imagine many thoughts were going through my mind. The first call I needed to make about this was to my wife, of course. Once I told Karen the news, she refused to believe it! "You're healthy, you're strong. This diagnosis is wrong. Who is this doctor?"

That made me think, "Why am I accepting this?"

Once I got home, I immediately went to my prayer closet, which is the library in my house. This is the place where I spend time with God every day. In this room, I have all the resources I need: Bibles, commentaries, over a hundred books on all kinds of spiritual topics that Karen and I have collected over the years. What I needed to find right now was one on healing. One of the many books I had on healing was *God's Creative Power for Healing* by Charles Capps, a very small paperback that's easy to read. I scrolled through the book and found a chapter called "God's Medicine." It was like a prescription. It said: "To be spoken by mouth three times a day until faith comes, then once a day to maintain faith. If symptoms and circumstances grow worse, double the dosage. There are no harmful side effects."

There are many scriptures in this book with declarations you can speak that address all kinds of issues. For instance, the immune system, healthy bones and marrow, growths, tumors, arthritis, and more. The one I found was for blood cells. One thing I learned is to be specific in your prayers and what you want to decree to happen. So the one I found that fit perfectly was based on Galatians 3:13, Mark 11:23, and Luke 17:6.

I didn't just read this declaration; I read it out loud, believed, and received it. It said: "I am redeemed from the curse. Galatians 3:13 is running, is flowing in my bloodstream. It flows to every cell in my body, restoring life and health (Mark 11:23; Luke 17:6)." I would repeat this over and over until I had it memorized. Every time the thought of the diagnosis came up, these words would immediately come out of my mouth. After a few days of this, I had almost completely forgotten about the diagnosis and continued on with my life. Karen and I refused to accept the news of leukemia.

January was always the annual 30 days of prayer at Oakland Church, so every evening, beginning at 6, Karen and I would make the 40-minute drive to church to gather for corporate prayer with other believers. Each day, Pastor Dominic would lead us to pray for certain things and then allow us to pray for our personal things as well. Some days, I would go and help in the TV department as I was a part of the TV ministry there. I did have the thought of maybe having someone pray for me about my diagnosis, but every time I thought about sharing with anyone, including the pastor, I just couldn't do it! I believed I didn't have it, so what should we even pray about? Besides, I didn't want anybody even saying, "Gerald has leukemia. Let's pray for him." This is how much I believed I didn't have it. I'm not saying you shouldn't have people praying for you. Having people supporting you and praying for you can be very important and powerful, but it's important that you pray and believe first.

February rolled around, and I had my appointment at Longevity Clinic. This would be the first time I would see her since my visit to the hematologist almost a month ago. She asked, "How was your visit?"

"It was horrible," I replied. "That doctor was so cold."

"I know. His bedside manner needs some work. I sent you there because he is the best!" Just what I needed to hear, that he's the best, after his diagnosis. Since she believed what he said might be true, she wanted to put me on additional vitamins and suggested I get an IV injection of vitamins once a month, which I agreed to. I told her I was scheduled to go back to see him in March, but I preferred to see a different doctor.

My reason was that a lot of my listeners worked at that office, and I would feel better going somewhere else where my name was not as familiar. So we chose an office about 45 minutes outside of Detroit for my next appointment on March 28th.

Around the same time, we were invited to go to Oral Roberts University with our friends, the Murrays, as they prepared their son, Isaac, for his orientation before entering the school in the fall of 2025. Our travel date to Oral Roberts was set for February 13th. A few days before our flight, a terrible snowstorm was about to hit our area, and it was likely that all flights would be canceled. Karen and I thought right then that we probably wouldn't go. Besides, was it that important to go to Oklahoma? This was all about Isaac, not us. After we discussed whether or not we would, I believe the Holy Spirit told me we needed to be there. So we booked the flight a day earlier to avoid the snowstorm.

The following Wednesday, we flew out to Tulsa. Sure enough, if we had waited, our flight would have been canceled. We began our tour of ORU and followed Isaac around through his orientation from building to building. I was amazed by the beautiful campus and by the students, faculty, and administration who were committed to keeping this a school of godly principles.

One building I was fascinated by was the Media Arts building. This brand-new building, completed in 2023, was state-of-the-art, featuring a beautiful theater. It also had sound studios, film editing suites, and a cutting-edge, state-of-the-art virtual film stage.

As Isaac, the Murrays, and Karen left to go to other parts of the campus, I decided to stick around in the film studio to see a few demonstrations of this huge video wall, which was truly amazing! I also got a chance to connect with a couple of instructors, share my project with them, and exchange information, with the possibility of using this amazing studio for some of my future projects.

While there, Karen called: "Hey, where are you? Meet us in the prayer tower."

"Okay, I'll be right there." The prayer tower sits right in the middle of ORU's campus. It's a five-story oval tower that overlooks the entire campus. It is said to be a place where Oral Roberts did much of his praying for the university, but it was also a place where students could go to have their quiet time with the Lord.

Entering the prayer tower, I was immediately surrounded by the peaceful sound of worship music. I looked around for Karen, who was with Ken and Beth Oswala, another couple from our group. I found them in a room with mood lighting and soft, tranquil worship music playing. A cross about my height sat in the middle of the room, lit with ambient lighting as if it glowed. The cross was filled with holes, so that you could write a prayer request on a small square of paper, roll it up, and stick it in one of the holes so any who came into the tower could pray over them.

For some reason, to me, this cross seemed very special as it had this heavenly glow to it, as if it were a burning bush. As the others were in the room, walking around, looking at the different statues and pictures on the wall, my eyes were fixed on this cross. I grabbed one of the small pieces of paper they had provided for prayer requests, and I wrote down my prayer for what I was believing for. You would think I would write down a prayer for my healing after being diagnosed with leukemia in the future, but I didn't. Probably because I never really believed I had it and hadn't given it any more thought. Instead, I wrote down that my movie, *The Rhythm*, would reach millions of people.

As I stuck my prayer request into one of the holes of the cross; the power of God was so strong! I immediately called Ken, Beth, and my wife over and joined hands with them and said, "We need to pray for your daughter Mattie." Mattie had been going through a divorce and a custody battle with her daughter, and I knew it was causing a lot of hurt to her, Ken, and Beth. So I was led to join hands with them and pray over the situation.

As I joined hands with them and began to pray over Mattie, the power of God seemed to get stronger and stronger! As I finished the prayer and we all let go of hands, the power was so strong that Ken and I fell on the floor and began to cry. I couldn't understand why I was crying so hard as I was on my knees. It seemed as though I was at the throne of God, and I couldn't look up or get up. I remember saying to the Lord as I felt so in awe to be in His presence, "Lord, forgive me. Just tell me what you want me to do. Whatever you need me to do, I'm here. I'm your servant. Just tell me."

As I am on the floor just crying uncontrollably, I remember Karen coming over and laying her hand on my back and asking, "Gerald, are you okay?" For a moment, I couldn't even answer her. I just continued to cry as the power kept me on my knees. Finally, after a few moments, I was able to get up, wondering what that was! Even as I write this, I'm still wondering if I can truly articulate what really happened to me that day and the impact that moment would have on me for the rest of my life, being in the presence of God like that, like never before. When we reunited with the others later that night, it would be the only thing I could talk about then and days later. I'm still blessed just thinking about it right now.

When we got back home, I got the news that my cousin Donna Kaye Sanders' condition of MS had now become ALS, and her health began to decline rapidly. Donna and I talked all the time, but now I couldn't reach her. The only way I could find out the latest about her condition was through her sister Paula, who informed me that matters were only getting worse.

At the same time, I also found out that my childhood friend was living his last days fighting prostate cancer, while another friend of the family, who was up in age, David Northcross, was confined to the hospital with only days to live.

Then there was Bobby Wright, Alana's father, whose cancer started to get more aggressive, which meant more emergency runs to the hospital. Each time, Alana would call me asking if I could meet the ambulance at the hospital so Bobby wouldn't be alone. A lot of times, when Bobby didn't answer the phone, Alana would ask if I could go by the apartment to check on him, which I would do. With these frequent visits to Bobby's apartment, I got to know him better. I found he was a well-educated person with a quick wit, always joking with the nurses who came in and out of his apartment.

Bobby loved shrimp, so I would always stop and get him a fried shrimp dinner and stay to talk with him. He would talk a lot about his life in California, the jobs he had, and life with him and Karen, which you would think would be a little awkward for him. But I didn't mind. I knew he needed the company, and his conversation wasn't anything derogatory, just places they lived and traveled, and life with Alana as a kid. I also found that Bobby had some great marketing skills from his past jobs, as he would offer me suggestions on promoting the movie and my radio show that made good sense!

Before our movie was released, I gave Bobby a copy to watch on his phone and asked if he would give me an honest critique. He was so excited! This made him feel like he was part of the process. He needed to feel some self-worth, and I realized I could help by giving him a small task to do for me. You see, Bobby refused to socialize with the senior assisted living community, which I always encouraged him to do, but I believe he was too weak to move the way he wanted to, so he spent most of his time in front of the TV watching the news, as I mentioned before. Each time I visited Bobby, I had the opportunity to share God's love with him in prayer and also bring books that he could read, and just continue to encourage him as he fought this disease.

In the span of three weeks in March, I would feel like the shadow of death would hover over my life like I had never seen before. Have you ever experienced back-to-back-to-back deaths in your family? This was the first time in my life when four close funerals would occur within a matter of days apart in March 2025.

First, my childhood friend Basil Sturtevant died. Then David Northcross would make his transition. Then, in Ripley, Tennessee, my close cousin Donna would pass away from ALS. Many times, I would ask, "Lord, why Donna?" Donna was like a sister to me. We had grown a lot closer in the later years of our lives and swore we would spend more time together. Donna is the reason I was inspired to write this book. She had called me one day, asking if I could jot down a few things about my life that she could put in a family scrapbook so that future generations would know who we are and the history of our family. As I started writing, I couldn't stop! So here I am writing the complete story.

Karen and I traveled to Ripley for Donna's homegoing, and it was so beautiful! Donna was a member of a sorority called Alpha Kappa Alpha (AKA). The church was packed with all of her sorority sisters dressed in pink and black, as was Donna. Each speaker had been picked by Donna. Being the leader with her personality, she had instructed them before she died how she wanted the funeral to flow without a lot of unnecessary comments, which we know can happen at funerals when it's open mic. I was on the list of speakers, and I was honored to play a role in this beautiful homegoing service.

Here is a portion of my speech:

Donna was like a sister to me, and more so, a sister in Christ. We would have many talks about spiritual things. She was always so encouraging to me, always telling me how God wanted to use me in so many ways and how His hand was on my life.

When she asked me to jot down a few things about me for a family album, I had no idea that I would be writing a book, but God had other plans. Thank you, Donna, for allowing God to use you not just for this but for the many ways that you have been a part of my life and many others. Your words of encouragement to me and many more will never be forgotten. I will never forget your smile, your joy, your contagious laughter, and the great times we have shared over the many years. You were more than just a cousin; you were a true sister in Christ. Now that you are with Christ in heaven, reunited with many of our family members who are also there in heaven, I know for a fact that you are hearing the words, "Well done, my faithful servant, well done!

After we returned home a few days later, we got the news that Bobby had been rushed to the hospital and was unconscious. When I got there, he was not responding at all. Of course, we immediately got on the phone with Alana and suggested that she get here right away. The next day, when she arrived, Bobby was even worse, now on a breathing machine. The doctors said he only has a few hours to live, and there was nothing they could do but keep him comfortable. It broke our hearts to see Alana at her dad's bedside, praying and hoping he would come out of this state, but he only seemed to slip further away. On his last day, his numbers seemed to decrease more and more as doctors and nurses reminded us that it could be any moment that he would make his transition. As Karen, Alana, Duke (Bobby's frat brother), and I grabbed hands, I began to pray.

"Father, we give You all of the praise and the glory. We thank You, Lord, because You are so worthy. Lord, right now we ask for Your peace and comfort that passes all understanding. We thank You that Bobby Wright will be in Your loving arms, where there is no pain, no sorrow. That he is with You in this beautiful place that is Your kingdom, where there are many mansions. We thank You that Your angels are in this room right now, surrounding Bobby, camping right here. Lord, we thank You that one day we will see him again. In the mighty name of Jesus. Amen."

Just as I had prayed that prayer, the breathing machine stopped with a long beep as the numbers zeroed out, as he made his transition. This was the first time in my life that I had ever prayed for someone while they were making their transition, and I would have never thought that I would be doing it for my wife's ex-husband. This was truly another special spiritual, emotional, unforgettable moment, getting to experience the presence of God and doing what He called us to do. This was truly a lesson in forgiveness, as things like this don't happen with ex-spouses. At Bobby's homegoing service, Alana asked if I would give the eulogy. Of course, I accepted and was honored.

In a matter of three weeks, four people who were close to me were laid to rest. I was reminded of this scripture in Psalms 23: "Yea, though I walk through the valley of the shadow of death, I will fear no evil; for You are with me; Your rod and Your staff, they comfort me."

At the end of March, I was scheduled for my appointment with the hematologist to get the results of a new blood test I had taken and given to a different doctor. This time it was in Macomb County, far out of metro Detroit, where I didn't have to worry about being recognized by any of my listeners. Sure enough, when I walked in, it was an office full of older white women, so I felt confident they wouldn't recognize my name as I signed in.

When my name was called, I went to the back and went through the regular procedures of weight and blood pressure, and then was placed in a room to await the doctor's entrance. As I sat there, the thoughts started to come up in my mind: "Is he going to confirm that I have leukemia?" As soon as that thought came up, I pulled my prayer on healing out of my pocket, and I read the paragraph that I would always read whenever these thoughts about this disease would pop up in my head: "I am redeemed from the curse. Galatians 3:13 is flowing through my bloodstream. It flows to every blood cell of my body, restoring life and health (Mark 11:23; Luke 17:6)." I said it out loud a few times before the doctor walked in.

When the doctor walked in, he was a lot friendlier than the previous doctor. He came in and closed the door. "Hey, Mr. McBride, how are you doing today?"

"Fine," I replied.

"Well, let me take a look." He goes through the normal procedure, looking in my eyes, checking my throat, ears, heartbeat, and so forth. Then he looks at the chart. Then he says, "Well, Mr. McBride, by the results of this test, your white blood cells look really good. They are normal. I don't see any issues at all. The other test must have been a fluke."

Right then, I could have jumped up and hugged him and praised God right in that room. But I decided to hold it in till I got outside and on the phone with my wife. The doctor suggested that we keep an eye on things and set up another appointment, which I was okay with. I shook his hand, thanked him, and went on my way. Once I got outside, I jumped for joy, praising God at the top of my lungs, and I skipped my way to the car. I called Karen and we praised God some more! On my way home, I couldn't help but think, Did my experience at the ORU prayer tower have anything to do with my healing? I never believed I had it and didn't talk about it or let anyone else, not giving it any value or attention. Is this part of the healing process, as I believe it says in Mark 11:23: "For assuredly, I say to you, whoever says to this mountain, 'Be removed and be cast into the sea,' and does not doubt in his heart, but believes that those things he says will be done, he will have whatever he says.'"

I was also told that, as I got closer to the ministry of filmmaking and what God has called me to do, the enemy would try to do everything he could to distract me and get me off track from my purpose. The deaths in the family, the diagnosis of death on me, and many other distractions were doing their best to stop me.

But here I am in May 2025, with the release of my first film, The Rhythm, now available on Amazon Prime, Apple TV, YouTube Movies, Roku, Tubi, Fandango at Home, Hoopla, and more streaming platforms, seen all over the world as I prayed, by millions. I am so thankful to God for this assignment that has been such a gratifying and wonderful journey and learning experience. We never stop growing and learning. I hope this book and the story of my journey inspire you to never give up on your dreams, no matter how old or young you are. It's never too late.

I encourage you to spend time with God, and He will speak to you. And when He does speak, please write it down. Shouldn't we document the words of the Creator of the universe? Start journaling. What an incredible privilege it is that He speaks to us.

Last, if you have a dream, don't be afraid to step out in faith. You are never too old or too young when God has put something on your heart. I never thought I could make a movie or write a book, but one day, I decided to take the first step. God cannot order your steps if you're unwilling to take any.

"The steps of a good man are ordered by the LORD: and he delighteth in his way. Though he fall, he shall not be utterly cast down: for the LORD upholdeth him with his hand" (Psalm 37:23-24). If you step in the wrong direction, He will point you back as long as you continue to acknowledge Him. "Trust in the LORD with all thine heart; and lean not unto thine own understanding. In all thy ways acknowledge Him, and He shall direct thy paths" (Proverbs 3:5-6).

But come to think of it, now my children, grandchildren, and future generations will know who I am and how God used my journey. I encourage you to share your story. It doesn't have to be long. Share your accomplishments, challenges, setbacks, battles, and victories. Your testimony can inspire others.

Last, always remember these timeless words: *"Don't be afraid, just believe."*

About the Author

Gerald McBride is a radio icon celebrating over 45 years in the broadcasting and production business. As CEO of Voice Over Productions (VOP), McBride is known across the USA as "The Man with the Golden Voice." Arguably one of the most successful voice-over talents in the Midwest, McBride is a voice-over and production master whose genius lies in his expert ability to combine the right music and creative message with each commercial spot.

As a youth growing up in Detroit under the influence of Motown and R&B music, he knew his passion for radio early on. Inspired and mentored by WJLB radio personality Donnie Simpson, he was encouraged to enter the business by becoming a "Soul Teen Reporter" for Mumford High School. In 1977, McBride enrolled in the Specs Howard School of Broadcasting, where he graduated and officially began his career in AM radio.

His broadcasting career has taken him to many stations, but in 1992, he settled in at WMXD 92.3 FM in Detroit, where he currently hosts his nationally syndicated *Old School House Party Radio Show* in over 30 markets. The urban show boasts as the #1 weekly radio show in all of its affiliate markets.

VOP is a full-service studio production company run by Gerald and his daughter Brandy Mitchell of Brandy Mitchell Design. They provide quality broadcast promotions specializing in movie trailers and commercials for Fortune 500 companies, high-profile celebrity clients, and concert promotion companies like AEG Live, Live Nation, North American Entertainment Group, Music Hall Center for the Performing Arts, Fox Theatre, and more. They have produced radio and TV commercials for Earth Wind & Fire, The Isley Brothers, Maze, The Jacksons, Stevie Wonder, Anita Baker, Kevin Hart, Chris Tucker, The Temptations, The O'Jays, The Whispers, Fantasia, and Fred Hammond, just to name a few.

Gerald McBride, a proud graduate of Mumford High School's class of 1975 and a multifaceted media professional, is now making waves in Hollywood with the release of his latest film, *Black Ice: The Rhythm*. As writer, producer, and director of the film, McBride brings his wealth of experience in voice-over, digital media production, and radio hosting to the silver screen.

Black Ice: The Rhythm is not only a cinematic achievement but also a testament to McBride's dedication to his roots and his commitment to inspiring the next generation. The film, shot against the backdrop of Detroit's iconic landmarks, tells the story of urban kids harnessing their innate talents to master the game of hockey, showcasing the resilience and creativity of Detroit's youth.

"Through *Black Ice: The Rhythm*, I aim to show young people that their dreams are within reach," says McBride. "It's about reminding them that regardless of where they come from, they have the power to achieve greatness with hard work and perseverance. *Black Ice: The Rhythm* is not just a movie; it's a movement. It's about harnessing the power of storytelling to uplift and inspire our community."

Gerald and his wife and best friend, Karen, have three grown children and two grandchildren. He is also a member of Oakland Church and is a true man of faith.

THE RHYTHM - A FILM BY GERALD MCBRIDE
www.therhythmmovie.com

The Rhythm film is an electrifying black hockey movie that follows the journey of Robert Taylor, a talented hockey player navigating the highs and lows of his career. Robert transforms a group of roller skaters into a championship-caliber ice-hockey team by harnessing their natural talent and passion, but they must confront racism and discrimination in the predominantly white world of the sport.

This movie, features a gripping story and intense action, and is often referred to as the jack black hockey movie or black ice hockey movie. With stunning visuals, powerful performances, and a storyline that highlights the strength of the human spirit, The Rhythm captures the hearts of viewers worldwide.

Don't miss out on this groundbreaking movie about hockey player Robert Taylor as he navigates the intense world of black ice hockey in The Rhythm. Watch it now in the comfort of your home - now streaming on Prime Video, Apple TV, Fandango, Roku, Google Play, Tubi, Hoopla, and YouTube.

"The Detroit Free Press says, "The Rhythm has a narrative about an underdog team that touches the emotion chords to 'Mighty Ducks' and 'The Karate Kid'."

OLD SCHOOL HOUSE PARTY WITH GERALD MCBRIDE
www.classicsouljams.com

The Old School House Party, hosted by Gerald McBride, is the only syndicated R&B oldies radio show that has consistently proven to be #1 in markets across the country.

Every weekend, Gerald turns up the energy for a five-hour celebration of the best old-school jams from the '70s, '80s, and '90s — packed with audience interaction, special features, and nonstop classic hits.

The show's signature segment, "The Battle of the Old School," pits two legendary artists or groups against each other in a head-to-head, song-for-song showdown. Listeners get to cast their votes and share their opinions on who truly reigns supreme.

As Gerald puts it, "The show feels like inviting all my friends over for a party and pulling out all my old LPs and 45s."

Tune in every weekend on stations nationwide and be part of the vibe that keeps generations grooving.

For more information, visit ClassicSoulJams.com.

VOICE OVER PRODUCTIONS
www.vopstudio.com

WHO WE ARE
WITH 30+ YEARS COMBINED EXPERTISE, VOP IS A ONE-STOP-SHOP FOR ADVERTISING, MULTI-MEDIA AND INTERACTIVE MARKETING EXPERIENCES..
Since 1989, VOP has connected with consumers through TV, radio and video promotions for some of the entertainment industry's most recognizable names. We use our expertise to capture the vision of you, our clients, and translate it into engaging, effective and memorable campaigns.

Our Brand Principles:
- Be CREATIVE
- Stay CURRENT
- Be ACCOMODATING
- Be RELIABLE
- Create work that is EFFECTIVE

WHAT WE DO
We are experts at creating unique, custom material and experiences that align with your brand's needs. This specialized approach means that we are strategic about the team, the goals and the plan of action that we recommend.

Our capabilities include:
- Video Production and Post Editing Services
- Voice Over Production
- Event Production
- Web Design
- Graphic Design